Language Hub

UPPER INTERMEDIATE
Student's Book A

Louis Rogers

macmillan
education

B2

Contents

Welcome

GRAMMAR
The passive

A Complete the sentences with the passive form of the verbs in the box.

> arrest   cancel   destroy   kill   release   take

1 Apparently, over 700,000 people _____ by mosquitos every year.
2 A decision _____ by the management board later in the week.
3 Three men _____ in connection with an attempted robbery in Soho last week.
4 The band's debut album _____ on 27th August 1991.
5 'We regret to inform passengers that the 7.36 to London King's Cross _____.'
6 Over 600 homes _____ in the forest fires that hit the area last month.

Zero, first and second conditionals

B Choose the correct options (a, b or c) to complete the conditional sentences.

1 If you don't hurry up, ___ the start of the film.
   a we'll miss   **b** we'd miss   **c** we'd have missed
2 Let me know if ___ any help with anything.
   a you'll need   **b** you need   **c** you'd need
3 If ___ the fire alarm, leave the building by the nearest exit.
   a you'll hear   **b** you'd heard   **c** you hear
4 I can't help you unless ___ me what's wrong.
   a you'd tell   **b** you tell   **c** you'd have told
5 If I had the money, ___ all my food there.
   a I'll buy   **b** I'd buy   **c** I'd have bought
6 If ___ Emily, I'll tell her to give you a call.
   a I see   **b** I'll see   **c** I'd see

VOCABULARY
Word formation

A Complete the sentences with the correct form of the words in brackets.

1 I thought that was a really _____ (product) meeting actually.
2 Just relax. Try not to _____ (think) it.
3 That reminds me, I need to _____ (new) my passport.
4 Sorry, but I think you may have _____ (understand) the question.
5 There's simply no _____ (science) evidence to support that.

Collocations

B Choose the correct options to complete the collocations.

1 We're sorry to announce that there are **serious** / **severe** delays on the central line.
2 Many new business owners find it difficult to **make** / **create** a profit in their first year.
3 I'm finding it really difficult to **stay** / **remain** motivated at the moment.
4 LeBron James has **made** / **given** the decision not to renew his contract with the Cleveland Cavaliers.
5 Scott seems pretty confident that his team will **reach** / **make** their target by June.
6 My brother-in-law actually **does** / **runs** a small business from home.
7 The government has **launched** / **released** a new campaign focussing on mental health.
8 Annoyingly, we got stuck in **serious** / **heavy** traffic on our way back.

C SPEAK Work in pairs. Discuss the questions.

1 What can you do to help stay motivated at work and in your studies?
2 Do you know anyone that runs a successful business? What do they do?
3 What's the most difficult decision you've ever made?

PRONUNCIATION
Intonation

0.1 **A** Draw arrows in the brackets to show whether the intonation rises (↗) or falls (↘) at each point in the sentences. Then listen and check.

1 Oh, really? (   ) Wow! That sounds great! (   )
2 It's a formal dinner, (   ) so it's important that you look smart. (   )
3 You've been to New York before, (   ) haven't you? (   )
4 Hmm … I'm not sure really. (   ) Maybe tomorrow afternoon? (   )
5 OK. (   ) I'll speak to Alicia and get back to you. (   )

Silent consonants

0.2 **B** Underline the silent consonants in each word. Then listen and check.

1 dishonest
2 listen
3 designer
4 climbing
5 muscle
6 knowledge

CONNECTIONS

> Friends show their love in times of trouble, not in happiness.
>
> Euripides

Women in a minimalist photo shoot in Copenhagen, Denmark.

OBJECTIVES

- talk about reactions and feelings
- design and present a meet-up group
- compare, contrast and summarise short biographies
- talk about people that have influenced you
- give your opinion on the role of inherited ability in success
- write a formal letter asking for information

Work with a partner. Discuss the questions.

1 Read the quote. Do you agree with Euripides? Why/Why not?

2 Can online relationships ever be as close as face-to-face relationships? Why/Why not?

3 What are the most important relationships in your life? Why?

1.1 Personality
- Talk about reactions and feelings
- Design and present a meet-up group

READING

A SPEAK Work in groups. Discuss the questions.

1 What qualities make someone a hero?

2 What type of people would you describe as 'everyday heroes'? Why?

3 Have you ever done anything heroic?

B SKIM FOR MAIN IDEAS Skim read *Inspiring stories of everyday heroes*. Choose the best summary (a or b) for each story. Use the information in the box to help you.

Skimming for the main ideas

Many modern articles, particularly those online, are presented in multiple short paragraphs to make them easier to read in a short amount of time. Often, we can understand the main ideas in this kind of article by quickly skimming the text.

1 a A man jumped onto the train tracks to save his baby.

   b A man jumped onto the train tracks to save a woman's baby.

2 a A young couple were saved from a forest fire that broke out in the fields they were driving through.

   b A young couple saved a family from a forest fire that spread to their house.

3 a A group of heroic pedestrians helped pull a schoolgirl out from under the car that had just hit her.

   b A driver heroically pulled a young schoolgirl out from under his car after an accident.

4 a Despite not being a strong swimmer, a young man was able to rescue his dog from strong currents at sea.

   b A passer-by was able to rescue a dog that had been swept out to sea.

C READ FOR DETAIL Read the article again and answer the questions. Underline the parts of the text that give you the answers.

1 What caused the buggy to start rolling towards the train tracks?

2 Was Jonas Neff in any real danger?

3 How did the fire develop so rapidly?

4 How did the children escape the burning building?

5 What had Becca Edwards been doing before the accident?

6 How did the driver react after the accident?

7 Why couldn't the dog get back to the beach?

8 Why was the rescuer so sure they could help?

D SPEAK Work in pairs. Discuss the questions.

1 How do you think you would react in the situations described in the article? Why?

2 Do you agree with Jonas Neff that he isn't a hero because 'anyone would do the same'? Why/Why not?

3 Why was Becca Edwards lucky that her accident happened on a main road?

Inspiring stories of EVERYDAY HEROES

BY EMILY FISCHER | OCT 15, 2018

In an age dominated by films about superheroes, it's good to know that we can all be heroes in the right context. To inspire you to do something next time you see someone in trouble, here are four real-life stories of normal people who jumped into action without a second thought.

BACK ON TRACK

Reactions are vital in everyday situations. Mother-of-one Christine Thomas was waiting on a crowded platform for her train home, when her phone rang. Expecting an important call, Christine rooted through her bag, not noticing that the brake on her child's buggy had failed and it was rolling towards the platform edge. She looked up, **horrified**, to see the buggy fall off the platform and onto the tracks below. Everyone on the platform froze, too **tense** to move, apart from Jonas Neff. Jonas jumped down quickly and lifted the buggy and child onto the platform, before pulling himself up just in time to avoid the oncoming train. Interviewed later by local radio, Jonas said, 'I'm not a hero. Anyone else would do the same.' Perhaps a little too modest considering that everyone else had been too shocked to move!

ESCAPING THE BLAZE

Everyone can be brave no matter how young or old they are. In the dry heat of summer, a fire started burning slowly in a farmer's field. As the winds became stronger, the fire spread quickly, surrounding the Sanchez family home. Trapped inside were a grandmother and her two young grandchildren. Spotting the danger as they were driving past, local residents Maria and Javier Hernandez stopped and got out to help. Maria later told local reporters '… I was so **impressed** by the character of such young children. They didn't know who we were but trusted us to catch them as they jumped from the top window. Once they were out, the grandmother jumped too.' The family were clearly upset to lose their home but equally **relieved** to all be alive.

THE STRENGTH OF MANY

Sometimes what you need is a whole group of heroes. **Thrilled** at having just won a local football tournament, 10-year-old Becca Edwards was cycling home from school one evening when she was hit by a car that had driven through a red light. The car stopped, trapping Becca underneath. **Devastated** by what had happened, the driver could do nothing as Becca screamed for help. Luckily for her, the accident took place on a busy main road. Nine pedestrians ran to help, working together to lift the car up just enough for a tenth hero to pull the schoolgirl out from underneath. Mark Benson, the first paramedic at the scene, said Becca was lucky to be alive and praised the quick response of the passers-by.

DANGER AT THE BEACH

Michael was happily throwing sticks into the sea for his dog, Linus, when suddenly it all went wrong. Strong currents dragged poor Linus out to sea and he wasn't able to swim back to shore. Terrified that Linus might die, but not a particularly strong swimmer, Michael stood helpless and **frustrated** on the beach. All of a sudden, a man came running past and dived into the water. After a brief struggle, he managed to pull Linus back to the shore where he was met with a huge round of applause from the crowd of onlookers that had gathered. 'Initially, I felt kind of **awkward** on the beach because I didn't know what to do' said the young hero. 'But I'm pretty confident in the water, so I just jumped in. I'm glad I could help out, but I wouldn't recommend swimming in such dangerous currents unless you're confident you can get back. A person's life is much more important than a dog's!'

VOCABULARY
Feelings

A Scan the article again. Complete the definitions with the adjectives in bold.

1 _____ feeling happy because something bad has stopped or hasn't happened

2 _____ feeling nervous, worried and not able to relax because of what might happen

3 _____ feeling embarrassed and not relaxed

4 _____ feeling very shocked and upset

5 _____ feeling very shocked or frightened

6 _____ feeling very pleased and excited

7 _____ feeling admiration for someone because of an unusually good achievement, quality or skill

8 _____ feeling annoyed or impatient because you can't do or achieve what you want

B Complete the sentences with adjectives from Exercise A.

1 I felt a bit _____ at first because I wasn't wearing a suit like everybody else.

2 I was just really _____ because the police wouldn't let me help.

3 It'd been a horrible flight and I was pretty _____ when the plane finally landed.

4 Firefighter Mark Cox was _____ to receive an award for bravery after the incident.

5 You couldn't help but be _____ by how quickly he reacted to the danger.

6 The crowd grew _____ as they waited to see if firefighters would reach the child in time.

7 I was _____ to hear that my grandmother had died as we were very close.

8 We were all _____ as the lift fell 15 floors towards the ground.

C Go to the Vocabulary Hub on page XVI.

D SPEAK Work in pairs. When was the last time you felt any of these emotions? What happened?

SPEAKING

SPEAK Work in groups. Read the scenarios (1–3) and discuss what you would do in each and why.

1 You're on a busy train when the woman in front of you suddenly falls over. Her eyes are closed and she doesn't appear to be breathing.

2 You're walking home late at night when you see a group of men shouting at a terrified businessman. You think they might attack him.

3 A fire breaks out in the house across the street. The old woman that lives there has difficulty walking and has poor hearing.

a

b

LISTENING

A SPEAK Work in pairs. Read the information about Get Together and discuss the questions.

1 What is the purpose of Get Together?

2 What kind of groups are available?

3 Do you think this is a good idea? Why/Why not?

Get Together

| Home | About us | Contact | | Login | Sign up |

Get Together helps connect millions of people with similar interests around the world. The basic idea is simple – find people in your local area that share your passion and form a group. Meet regularly to play together, learn new skills or just make new friends.

Our members have rediscovered their passion for reading, trained for triathlons, even changed their careers – the possibilities are endless. Whatever you're interested in, you're sure to find a group that suits you.

Members	Groups	Countries
25 million	185,967	148

B LISTEN FOR MAIN IDEAS Listen and match the conversations (1–3) to the pictures (a–c).

1.1

Conversation 1 ___   Conversation 2 ___   Conversation 3 ___

C LISTEN FOR DETAIL Listen again. Are these sentences true (T) or false (F)? Correct the false sentences.

1.1

1 a Both speakers at the ukulele group regularly go to meet-ups. *T / F*

   b They have played the ukulele for the same amount of time. *T / F*

2 a The man's flat is in a convenient location. *T / F*

   b The man has done a 10K race before. *T / F*

3 a Martin needs to return the registration form as soon as possible. *T / F*

   b Martin and Yumi both enjoyed the Haruki Murakami novel *Norwegian Wood*. *T / F*

D SPEAK Work in groups. Discuss the questions.

1 What are the benefits of joining a group like this?

2 Do you think this is the best way to meet new people in your area? Why/Why not?

3 What Get Together groups would you like to join in your area? Why?

GRAMMAR
Question forms

A Listen to extracts from the conversations again. Complete the questions.

1.2

1 **Sarah:** Yeah, same really. It just seemed like a fun thing to do. Anyway, _____ _____ the group tonight?

   Mark: Er, Lucy, I think. She's actually a professional musician, so we're in good hands.

2 **Fyodor:** Well, I like Clapham, but my flat is a really long way from the station and I don't really get on with my flatmates.

   Alana: Oh, fair enough. _____ _____ like them?

   Fyodor: Well, one of them works night shifts so he always comes home really late and the other just spends all his time in his room.

3 **Fyodor:** I suppose so. Who _____ _____?

   Alana: A couple of friends I've known since university. They can definitely be annoying sometimes, but I wouldn't want to live with anyone else.

4 **Martin:** Excuse me, _____ _____ where I sign in for the book club Get Together?

   Yumi: Er, yeah, right here actually. I'm running the group tonight. Can I take your name, please?

C

PRONUNCIATION
Intonation in *yes/no* and *wh-* questions

A Listen to the questions from the conversations.

1.3 Draw arrows to show whether the intonation rises (↗) or falls (↘) at the end of each question.

1 Have you been playing long? ___

2 Where were you living before? ___

3 Who do you live with? ___

4 Have you had time to finish the book yet? ___

B Circle the arrows to predict which intonation will be used

1.4 in each question. Then listen and check.

1 Is there an application fee? [↗] / [↘]

2 What kind of event could we run? [↗] / [↘]

3 How often does the group meet? [↗] / [↘]

4 Do you need any special equipment? [↗] / [↘]

5 Is everyone happy with that? [↗] / [↘]

B WORK IT OUT Choose the correct options to complete the rules.

Question forms

Indirect questions

We use indirect questions when we want to be more polite. They often start with phrases like *Could you tell me …?*, *Do you know …?* and *Would you mind …?* In indirect questions, we use the same word order as a statement (i.e. ¹*verb + subject / subject + verb*) and we don't use the auxiliary *do*.

Questions with prepositions

If a verb is followed by a preposition, the preposition comes at the ²*beginning / end* of the sentence.

Subject questions

When we ask about the subject of a sentence, we use the same word order as a statement, and the question word (e.g. *when, who, what, which,* etc) replaces the ³*subject / object*.

Negative questions

When we ask negative *wh-* questions, we ⁴*use / don't use* the auxiliary verb, even in subject questions.

C Go to the **Grammar Hub** on **page VI**.

D PRACTISE Reorder the words to make questions.

1 would / most like to meet / which / you / famous person

_____ ?

2 is / can / ask / your earliest memory / I / what

_____ ?

3 think / you / is more important / diet or exercise / do

_____ ?

4 English / you / why / are / studying

_____ ?

5 your job / what / like about / you / don't

_____ ?

E SPEAK Work in pairs. Discuss the questions in Exercise D.

SPEAKING HUB

A PLAN Work in groups. Brainstorm a list of things you like doing or are interested in.

B PREPARE Choose one of your ideas from Exercise A to use as the focus of a new meet-up group. Make notes about:

- what you'll actually do at the meet-ups
- where / how often you'll meet
- what special events you might organise
- how much members will need to pay and why

C PRESENT Present your ideas to the class. Ask other groups follow-up questions to get more information.

D DISCUSS As a class, discuss which meet-up groups would work best in your area and why.

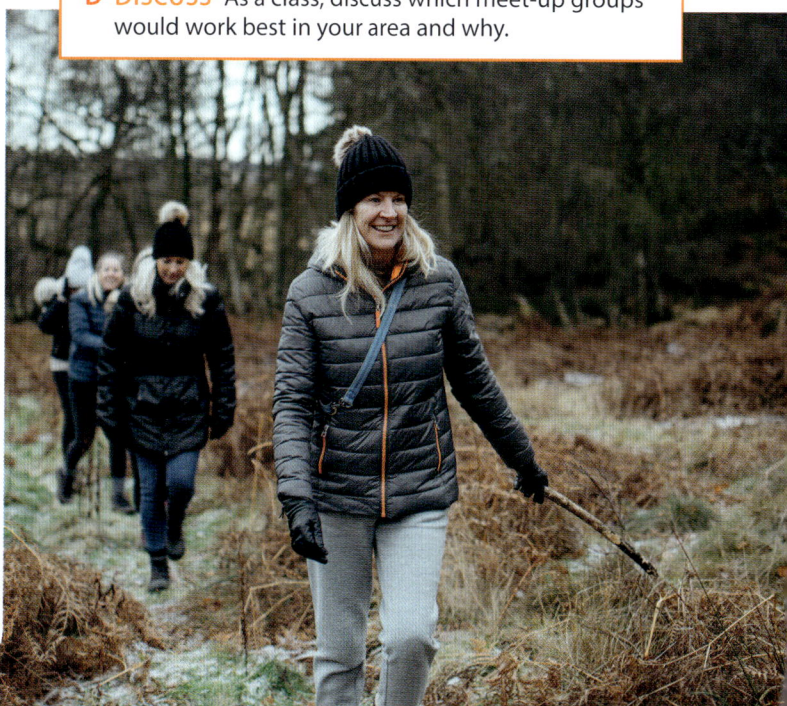

○– **Talk about reactions and feelings**
○– **Design and present a meet-up group**

1.2 Who we are

- Compare, contrast and summarise short biographies
- Talk about people that have influenced you

G tense review
V personality adjectives; noun suffixes
L listening for the main ideas
P connected speech: final consonant and initial vowel

READING

A SPEAK Work in groups. What do you know about the people in the article below?

B READ FOR GIST Read *The long road to success* and choose the sentence (1–3) that best describes the connection between the two people.

1 famous people that had difficult childhoods
2 famous people that overcame challenges to succeed
3 famous people that failed at university

C SCAN Scan the article again and tick (✓) the person that each sentence is about.

Which person …	Stephen Hawking	Vera Wang
1 had an unusual childhood?		
2 didn't meet their academic potential?		
3 had a significant change in their career?		
4 was inspired to start a new business?		
5 lived much longer than people expected?		
6 is very rich and successful today?		

The long road to success

It's easy to think that the rich and famous have always lived a privileged life, but many have overcome great adversity to get to where they are today. When life presents us with challenges, how we react can determine how successful we become.

Stephen Hawking

What was his early life like?
Keeping bees in the basement of their crumbling St. Albans home, making fireworks in the greenhouse and driving around in a former London taxi, the Hawking family was certainly a little eccentric. In fact, they often ate dinner in silence [1] while each of them was reading a book.

Was he always a gifted academic?
At school, Hawking was thought of as bright but not brilliant. In his first year of secondary school, [2] he was the third worst student in the class. He also admitted to being a lazy student at Oxford University, only spending about an hour a day studying.

When did his condition develop?
Hawking first recognised something was wrong when he started to occasionally trip and fall while studying for a PhD at Cambridge University. At 21 years old, he was diagnosed with amyotrophic lateral sclerosis (ALS), and given just two years to live.

How did this affect him?
Hawking said that before he was diagnosed with ALS, he had been bored with life. Being told that he would not live to complete his PhD encouraged the young physicist to focus on his studies.

What made him famous?
Hawking is most famous for his research into black holes. By his early thirties, he had won many awards and went on to publish numerous papers and books, including *A brief history of time*. He was still proposing groundbreaking ideas about space and time until his death 50 fifty years later.

Glossary

ALS (n) amyotrophic lateral sclerosis is a serious disease that affects nerve cells and causes muscles to become smaller and weaker

Vera Wang

Did she always want to work in fashion?
From the age of eight years old, Wang wanted to become a professional figure skater. After years of training and competing, she realised that no matter how hard she trained, she would never make the Olympic team. She gave up figure skating and moved to Paris to study Art History. It was there in the French capital that Wang realised she wanted to pursue a career in the fashion industry. After [3] she had completed her year abroad, Wang moved back to the USA where she worked as a sales assistant at Yves Saint Laurent. It was at this point she met *Vogue* fashion director Frances Stein, who told Wang to give her a call when she graduated. A year and a half later she did, and spent the next 17 years working as an editor at the magazine.

How did she get into fashion design?
Wang left *Vogue* in 1982 and lived in Paris for several years before taking up a position as design director at Ralph Lauren in New York. When planning her wedding in 1989, she was so disappointed by the lack of fashionable wedding dresses that she decided to design her own. A year later, she opened her own bridal shop, from which [4] she has built a fashion empire worth millions.
[5] Today, she is worth over $600 million and is considered one of America's most successful self-made millionaires. Her clothes are worn by everyone from Michelle Obama to Kim Kardashian. She remains heavily involved in her company and is known for working long hours and holding frequent meetings to ensure she knows [6] exactly what's happening.

D READ FOR DETAIL Read again. Complete the sentences with no more than two words from the article.

1 Stephen Hawking was considered a _____ student at university.

2 Before finding out about his illness, he only studied for _____ each day.

3 He was told he would live for just _____ more years.

4 He was given a lot of _____ for his early work.

5 Vera Wang gave up her dream of becoming a professional _____ after realising she would never make the Olympic team.

6 She worked as a _____ before joining Vogue shortly after graduation.

7 She left Vogue in 1982, after _____ _____ working as an editor.

8 Her personal fortune is thought to be more than _____.

E SPEAK Work in pairs. Can you think of anyone else that has overcome huge challenges in order to succeed?

GRAMMAR
Tense review

A Scan the article again. Match the highlighted sentences (1–6) to the tenses below.

___ present simple ___ past continuous

___ past simple ___ present continuous

___ past perfect ___ present perfect

B WORK IT OUT Complete the rules with the tenses in Exercise A.

Tense review

We use the ¹_____ to talk about past states or completed actions in the past.

We use the ²_____ to talk about things happening now or around now.

We use the ³_____ to talk about a state or action that started in the past and is still happening now.

We use the ⁴_____ to talk about something that is generally true.

We use the ⁵_____ to talk about an action in the past that was in progress when something else happened.

We use the ⁶_____ to talk about a past action that occurred before another past action.

C Go to the **Grammar Hub** on **page VI**.

D PRACTISE Complete the text with the correct form of the verbs in brackets.

Saroo Brierley

Saroo Brierley ¹_____ (be) born in Ganesh Talai, a suburb in Khandwa, India. His family was poor and often had to beg for food and money. When he was five, Saroo ²_____ (take) a train with his older brother, Ghuddu, from Khandwa to the city of Burhanpur, where Ghuddu had a job cleaning trains at night. By the time they arrived, Saroo was so tired he fell asleep on the platform. Ghuddu told him to wait there but when he ³_____ (not return), Saroo grew impatient and got on a train that ⁴_____ (wait) at the platform. He fell asleep and when he woke up, he realised that he ⁵_____ (travel) to Kolkata by mistake – 1500 km away from home.

After living on the streets for three weeks, he got a place in a local orphanage. An Australian family adopted him and he ⁶_____ (spend) the next 25 years living in Australia. Saroo wanted to find his family. Using his memories and Google Earth, Saroo eventually ⁷_____ (find) his hometown in India.

Before his story was turned into an internationally successful book and film, Saroo ⁸_____ (help) his dad run a business. Now he ⁹_____ (work) as a motivational speaker until he decides what to do next. Since living in Australia, Saroo ¹⁰_____ (have) a happy life and always feels lucky.

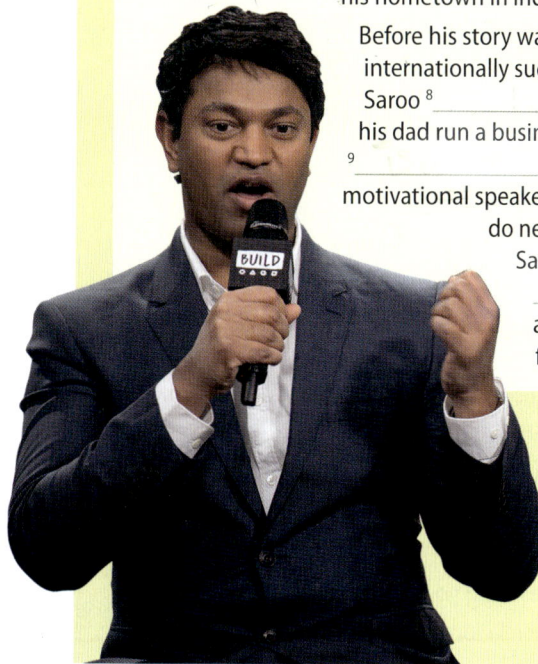

E SPEAK Work in pairs. Discuss the questions.

1 What challenges do you have in your life at the moment?

2 What is the biggest challenge you have ever faced? How did you deal with it?

SPEAKING

A PREPARE Student A – Go to the **Communication Hub** on **page XX**. Student B – Go to the **Communication Hub** on **page XXII**.

B SPEAK Tell your partner about the person you read about.

C DISCUSS Work in groups. Discuss the questions.

1 What are the similarities between the two people you read about?

2 Who do you think had bigger challenges to overcome? Why?

LISTENING

A SPEAK Work in pairs. Tell your partner about your closest friends. How are they similar/different? Is it important to have different types of friends? Why/Why not?

🔊 1.5 **B LISTEN FOR MAIN IDEAS** Listen to an interview about friendship, personality and success. Put the following topics in the order they are discussed. Use the information in the box to help you.

> ### Listening for the main ideas
>
> Talks, speeches and interviews usually contain multiple main ideas, based around one central theme. Speakers often introduce each new idea or point with phrases such as *the next is*, *another one is*, *the last is*, etc. Identifying these phrases can help you focus on the key information that follows.

___ a work colleague who makes you laugh

___ a complete opposite to you

___ a best friend you can rely on

___ a very honest friend who tells you the truth

___ a neighbour in your community

___ a friend who is not afraid

🔊 1.5 **C LISTEN FOR DETAIL** Listen to the interview again. Choose the correct options (a, b or c) to complete the sentences.

1 According to research, we can only maintain a friendship group of …
   a several hundred people.
   b no more than 50 people.
   c no more than 20 people.

2 Open-minded adventurers are people who …
   a are always making new friends.
   b don't find new situations stressful.
   c like habit and routine.

3 It's important to have a friend who …
   a will constantly praise you.
   b is very flexible.
   c will be brutally honest with you.

4 Moving a lot affects our relationships with …
   a our neighbours.
   b our colleagues.
   c our relations.

5 Successful people …
   a prioritise work over everything else.
   b work longer hours than their colleagues.
   c feel part of a group.

D SPEAK Work in groups. Discuss the questions.

1 What positive and negative effects does social media have on our relationships?

2 How well do you know your neighbours/colleagues/classmates? Do you consider any of them friends?

VOCABULARY
Personality adjectives

🔊 1.6 **A** Complete the extracts with the personality adjectives in the box. Then listen and check.

| arrogant down-to-earth easy-going loyal |
| open-minded self-centred stubborn witty |

1 We all need a _____ best friend. Someone who will support us no matter what happens.

2 This person is an _____ adventurer. They always force us into new and different situations.

3 They are _____ and open to new ideas, cultures and activities. None of these things stress them out.

4 No, these people aren't _____. They just have a lot of self-belief.

5 They'll tell you when you're being _____ and should think about others more.

6 Or they'll tell you you are being _____ and need to be more flexible.

7 She's very _____. She just does everything in this very sensible, practical way. I guess she is a helpful person to have around!

8 Having no _____ people to have a laugh with would make work very boring.

B Choose the correct adjectives to complete the sentences.

1 My neighbour is really *easy-going / open-minded*. He's always willing to consider new ideas or opinions.

2 In a difficult situation, she stays calm. She's so *loyal / down-to-earth* and knows exactly what to do.

3 She never gets stressed. She's so *easy-going / witty*.

4 I find her really *arrogant / self-centred*. It's like she thinks she is better than everyone.

5 Even when I've done stupid things, she has always been *loyal / down-to-earth* and supported me.

6 There's no point arguing with him. He's just so *stubborn / arrogant* and won't change his mind.

7 I think she's really *easy-going / witty* actually. She's always making clever jokes.

8 Stop being so *self-centred / stubborn*. Try to think about other people for once!

C Go to the Vocabulary Hub on page XVII.

D Complete the personality quiz.

What kind of person are you?

Rate yourself on a scale of 1–5.
1 = Strongly disagree 5 = Strongly agree

You find it easy to stay focused even when you are under pressure. 1 2 3 4 5

You usually start conversations. 1 2 3 4 5

You rarely do something just out of curiosity. 1 2 3 4 5

You feel more important than other people. 1 2 3 4 5

Getting what you want is more important than keeping others happy. 1 2 3 4 5

Making other people laugh is important to you. 1 2 3 4 5

You try to win arguments even when you might be wrong. 1 2 3 4 5

You don't believe in hiding your feelings to keep people happy. 1 2 3 4 5

E **SPEAK** Work in pairs. Describe your partner's personality using their answers to the quiz in Exercise D. Do you agree with their description of you?

PRONUNCIATION
Connected speech: final consonant and initial vowel

A Listen to the sentence and draw (‿) between any words that link together.

1.7

Most people spend at least 50 per cent of their waking hours at work.

B Work in pairs. Look at the example in Exercise A and discuss the questions.

1 Does the first word end in a consonant or a vowel sound?

2 What sound does the next word begin with?

C Read the sentences. Draw (‿) to predict which words are connected. Then listen and check.

1.8

1 They are open-minded and friendly.

2 She achieved a lot despite having a difficult childhood.

3 He built a successful business at a young age.

4 We spent a lot of our time together going for walks in the countryside.

5 We hung out at the beach, went out at night and played games online together.

VOCABULARY

Noun suffixes

We use the following suffixes to change adjectives to nouns:

-ion (e.g. *ambitious > ambition*)

-ity/-ty (e.g. *flexible > flexibility*)

-ence (e.g. *different > difference*)

-ness (e.g. *stubborn > stubbornness*)

-ism (e.g. *pessimistic > pessimism*)

Complete the sentences with the noun form of the adjectives in brackets. Use the information in the box to help you.

1 I think what I value most in a friend is _____ _____ (*loyal*).

2 _____ (*optimistic*) is a great quality for a close friend to have.

3 Her _____ (*determined*) to succeed had a great influence on me.

4 Frankly, I was amazed by his _____ (*arrogant*).

5 She took _____ (*responsible*) for her actions.

6 He always gave me the _____ (*confident*) to try new things.

SPEAKING HUB

A **PREPARE** Make a list of people that have had a big influence on you (e.g. a teacher, your best friend, a grandparent, etc).

B **PLAN** Choose one of the people in Exercise A to tell your partner about. Use the following questions to make notes:

1 What was their personality like?

2 Why did they have such an influence on you?

3 What things did you do together?

C **SPEAK** Work in pairs. Use your notes from Exercise B to talk about the person you chose. Ask follow-up questions to find out more about them.

D **DISCUSS** As a class, discuss the types of people that influenced you. What personality traits do they share?

○– **Compare, contrast and summarise short biographies**

○– **Talk about people that have influenced you**

Café Hub

▶ The Special Olympics

COMPREHENSION

A Work in pairs. Successful athletes are often not the only person in their family to compete at the highest level. Why do you think this is?

B ▶ Watch a news report about a competitor at the Special Olympics. The report focuses on this person because …

1 he is competing at the highest level in his sport.

2 his great grandfather was also a successful athlete.

3 he is competing in multiple events.

C ▶ Watch again. Complete the sentences with no more than three words from the report.

1 Daniel Wolff won the _____ event at the Special Olympics in 2015.

2 His great grandfather won a _____ at the Berlin Olympics in 1936.

3 Daniel's grandfather describes his achievement as '_____'.

4 This year's Special Olympics has drawn crowds of _____ people.

5 _____ people in Daniel's family have come to watch him compete.

D ▶ Are these sentences true (T) or false (F)? Correct the false sentences. Then watch the report again to check.

1 Daniel's grandfather believes that sporting ability is genetic. *T / F*

2 Daniel was confident before the event that he would win. *T / F*

3 The reporter believes Daniel had a good level of support at the event. *T / F*

4 His father didn't think it was fair to leave his children at home. *T / F*

5 The 400 metres is the only event Daniel is taking part in. *T / F*

AUTHENTIC ENGLISH

A Work in pairs. Read the extract from the report. What do you think the expression in bold means?

> Daniel Wolff crosses the line to win the 400 metres and shows that athletic success really can **run in the family**.

B Read the information in the box and check your answer to Exercise A. Why is this idiom appropriate for the report?

> **Idioms: family**
>
> Idioms are a group of words whose meaning is different from the meaning of the individual words. As this can make them difficult to remember, one way to record new idioms is to group them by topic. Some common idioms in English are connected to the topic of family:
>
> *You have to choose your brother. Remember – **blood is thicker than water**!* (= used to say that family relationships are always more important than any others)
>
> *Athletic ability **runs in the family** – both he and his father played for their country.* (= if an ability, quality, disease, etc runs in the family, many family members have it)

C Read the sentences (1–3) and try to guess the meaning of the idioms in bold.

1 His grandfather was also a famous author – writing must **be in the blood**.

2 She **followed in her** mother's **footsteps** and trained to become a doctor.

3 He **is the spitting image of** his father at that age.

D Work in pairs. Discuss the questions.

1 Do you think any of your skills, abilities, etc are in your blood?

2 Have you followed in the footsteps of anyone in your family?

3 Have you ever been told you are the spitting image of someone?

▶ Family matters

SAM MALCOLM AMANDA HARRY EMILY

A Work in pairs. What job do you have now or want to have in the future? What makes you particularly suitable for it?

B ▶ Watch the video. What runs in Harry's family? What runs in Sam's family?

SPEAKING SKILL

A ▶ Watch the video again and complete the extracts from the conversation.

Sam: And I must remember to get the paper towels for the toilets.
1 _____, did the hand soap arrive in the delivery?

Sam: I'm just so excited about getting this new café off the ground – I don't want to forget anything. Anyway, how are you getting on?

Sam: Oh really? You're not going to blame your upbringing are you?

Harry: 2 _____ because untidiness really does run in my family. I mean, you should have seen the state of our house when I was growing up!

Sam: 3 _____ things that run in the family, I actually saw this really heartwarming story on the news …

B Work in pairs. Discuss the questions. Then read the information in the box to check your answers.

1 What is the function of the phrases you wrote in Exercise A?

2 What is different about *anyway*?

Developing and introducing new topics

Developing topics

During a conversation, a speaker may say something that reminds us of relevant information or a related topic. To introduce our idea, we can use the following expressions:
Speaking/Talking of which …, Talking of [topic] …, Actually, that reminds me of …, Strange you should mention that (because) …

Introducing new topics

We use *anyway* to introduce a completely unrelated topic.
Anyway, I think we should …

C Work in pairs. Student A – Talk about one of the topics below. Student B – Listen and either develop or change the topic. Then swap roles.

- a film that you saw recently
- a news item you read recently
- a restaurant you went to recently
- an interesting thing that happened to you recently
- a journey you went on recently
- a sporting event you saw recently

SPEAKING HUB

A **PREPARE** Work in pairs. Brainstorm a list of factors that affect our abilities and skills.

B **PLAN** Work in two groups. You are going to debate the following:

Practice has no effect on ability – we inherit our abilities from our parents.

Group A – You agree with the idea above.

Group B – You disagree with the idea above.

Plan your arguments. Think about how to support your position, as well as what the other group might say.

C **SPEAK** Hold your debate.

D **REFLECT** Which group put forward the more persuasive argument? Which side do you agree with?

○─ **Give your opinion on the role of inherited ability in success**

➤ Turn to page XXIV to learn how to write a formal letter asking for information.

VOCABULARY

A Choose the correct options (a, b or c) to complete the sentences.

1 They were ___ to arrive at the airport just in time for their flight.

   a relieved   b devastated   c furious

2 I was completely ___ when we lost the World Cup final on penalties.

   a thrilled   b relieved   c devastated

3 Louis was ___ to find out his daughter had been offered a place at Cambridge University.

   a disgusted   b thrilled   c horrified

4 I'm pretty ___ by your lack of enthusiasm.

   a frustrated   b impressed   c relieved

5 Everyone sat in ___ silence as I broke the bad news.

   a relieved   b disgusted   c stunned

B Complete the sentences with the adjectives in the box.

| easy-going   loyal   optimistic   sensitive   stubborn   witty |

1 Why does he have to be so _____ all the time? Not everything in life is good!

2 This girl I met at the party was so _____. I was laughing all night!

3 I don't think I've ever seen him get stressed or upset. He's so _____.

4 The club has a lot of _____ supporters. They're still buying tickets – even at £120 a game!

5 Stop being so _____ and just admit that you're wrong!

6 How can we break the news to her? She's such a _____ person.

C Complete the text with the correct form of the words in brackets.

Perfectionism

Do you find it hard to live up to your own [1]_____ (*expect*)? Do you experience [2]_____ (*frustrate*) when you work with lazy people? If so, you might be a perfectionist. The positive thing about working with a perfectionist is their [3]_____ (*reliable*), [4]_____ (*dedicate*) and [5]_____ (*professional*). However, if you are a perfectionist, don't assume everyone will want to work with you because of these characteristics. Your constant criticism of other people can affect their [6]_____ (*confident*). Your [7]_____ (*stubborn*) and inability to admit you might be wrong are not attractive either. You probably won't be worried about that, though, as you're likely to be convinced of your own [8]_____ (*superior*).

GRAMMAR

A Choose the correct options to complete the sentences.

1 Could you tell me *where is the reception desk / where the reception desk is*, please?

2 So why *didn't you / you didn't* like the film?

3 Really? So, *what was happening / what happened* then?

4 Who *Javier is meeting / is Javier meeting*?

5 Which candidate *are you going to vote for / are you going to vote*?

6 Why *you don't come / don't you come* out this evening?

7 *You haven't / Haven't you* finished the homework yet?

8 Do you mind telling me *how old you are / how old are you*?

9 Can I ask what you think *you are doing / are you doing*?

10 Why *you are so / are you so* worried about it?

B Complete the conversations with the correct form of the words in brackets.

1 **A:** _____ (*you / ever / be*) to Japan?

   B: Yes, I actually _____ (*teach*) English in Tokyo for three years after university.

2 **A:** _____ (*you / know*) Yara?

   B: Yes, I _____ (*know*) her since university.

3 **A:** Why _____ (*be / you*) at work today? I thought you had an important meeting.

   B: I _____ (*have*) a tough week, so I decided to take a day off.

4 **A:** What _____ (*you / do*) when you heard the news?

   B: I _____ (*just / put*) Mia to bed when my brother phoned.

5 **A:** _____ (*you / find*) a new job yet?

   B: Maybe. I actually _____ (*have*) an interview last week.

6 **A:** Where _____ (*you / go*) when you had the accident?

   B: I _____ (*drive*) to work.

7 **A:** Oh no! My yoga class _____ (*start*) in five minutes and I can't find my mat!

   B: Calm down. Try to think. Where _____ (*you / last / see*) it?

8 **A:** I kept getting lost when I _____ (*go*) to Berlin last week.

   B: It's difficult to learn your way around a place you _____ (*never / go*) to before.

LIFESTYLES

Plunge boldly into the thick of life, and seize it where you will, it is always interesting.

Johann Wolfgang von Goethe

Underwater view of a boy jumping into a swimming pool.

OBJECTIVES

- talk about health and lifestyle choices
- plan and conduct a lifestyle survey
- conduct an interview about lifestyle changes
- debate the impact of smartphones
- give your opinion on food choices
- write an article giving advice

Work with a partner. Discuss the questions.

1 Read the quote. What do you think Goethe means? Do you agree with him? Why/Why not?

2 Do you dive into the unknown or do you play it safe?

3 What is most important to you in life?

2.1 A full life
● Talk about health and lifestyle choices
● Plan and conduct a lifestyle survey

V — health and fitness
L — listening for reasons
G — present perfect simple and present perfect continuous
P — connected speech: present perfect continuous

VOCABULARY
Health and fitness

A SPEAK Work in pairs. Brainstorm a list of things that have positive or negative effects on our health.

B Complete the definitions (a–f) with the words in bold.

1 A lack of healthy lunch options has led to worrying levels of child **obesity**.

2 Drinking a lot of coffee can cause **anxiety** and negatively affect sleep.

3 Fatty foods like butter and cheese can increase levels of **cholesterol**.

4 She suffered from **depression** after losing her job.

5 There are around 500 **calories** in an average slice of chocolate cake.

6 My husband's been under a lot of **stress** at work recently.

a _____ (n) a unit for measuring how much energy you get from food

b _____ (n) a type of fat in the blood that can cause heart disease if you have too much

c _____ (n) a condition in which someone is too fat in a way that is dangerous for their health

d _____ (n) a medical condition in which a person is so unhappy they cannot live a normal life

e _____ (n) pressure or worry caused by problems in everyday life

f _____ (n) the feeling of being very worried that something bad is going to happen

C Complete the sentences with words from Exercise B.

1 I suffer a lot from _____ in the winter. I'm much more positive in the summer months.

2 Keeping your diet low in fatty foods can help lower _____.

3 Nuts have more _____ in them than you might think.

4 _____ is a huge problem in my country. Nearly a quarter of people are dangerously overweight.

5 _____ is one of my biggest issues. I worry so much about everything.

6 I worry about my _____ levels. I'm under too much pressure at work.

D Go to the **Vocabulary Hub** on **page XVII**.

E SPEAK Work in pairs. What effects do the following have on our health?

- junk food
- smoking
- lack of exercise
- poor work–life balance

READING

A PREDICT Work in pairs. Look at the pictures (1–6) and the corresponding sub-headings in the article. Discuss how you think each of these things might help people to live longer.

B SCAN Read *Six ways to live longer* and check your predictions from Exercise A.

C READ FOR DETAIL Read the article again and answer the questions. Underline the parts of the text that give you the answers.

1 Why might owning a pet be good for your physical health?

2 What is different about the Japanese diet?

3 Why do people who think about details tend to live longer?

4 What charitable activity can help you live longer?

5 What does singing reduce?

6 What don't negative people pay attention to?

D SPEAK Work in pairs. Discuss the questions.

1 Why do you think owning a dog might reduce the risk of heart disease?

2 Why do you think 'smaller plates' have a positive effect on Japanese health?

3 Which of the suggested lifestyle changes in the text would you be happy to make? Why?

4 What other changes could you make to improve your overall health?

1

SIX WAYS | TO LIVE LONGER

For the first time, people are expected to live a shorter life than their parents. Higher levels of obesity, a reliance on processed foods and more sedentary lifestyles are all taking their toll. If we want to live longer and healthier lives, there are many things we can do to slow the ageing process and it doesn't just involve eating more healthily and going to the gym.

1 GET A PET

If exercise isn't your thing, then perhaps you should consider getting a pet. Scientists in Sweden found that people who owned a dog had a much lower risk of various heart diseases and other illnesses. Dogs obviously need walking but having a pet is also good for many mental health issues such as lowering stress, fear and anxiety.

2 MOVE TO JAPAN

A dramatic solution would be to move countries. The Japanese lifestyle is arguably much healthier than in many other countries. Firstly, they eat a lot less fat and lower their cholesterol by eating less dairy and swapping red meat for fish. They also make healthier food choices by eating seaweed, lots of vegetables and by eating fewer **processed foods**. They use smaller plates and have a lower **calorie** intake than most other countries. Therefore, Japan has a very low obesity rate, with just under 4% of the population considered obese.

3 THINK OF THE DETAILS

People who think carefully about everything and pay a lot of attention to detail tend to live longer. Those who are careful with money, put everything in its right place and focus on details don't comfort eat as much as other people, and sleep better. People who carefully think things through deal better with stress and generally see the positives in most situations. They also have less risky lifestyles.

4 HELP OTHERS

In general, having strong social ties is a good predictor for living a longer and healthier life. People who take care of others are much more likely to make and keep friends throughout their life. Not only will you feel better if you help others but you will also live longer. A study in the USA found that people who volunteer regularly in their lifetime live significantly longer than those who don't.

5 SING

People who regularly sing, especially in groups, tend to have a longer life expectancy. Researchers at Harvard and Yale universities in the USA found that singing in a choir makes you happier and healthier than others. Singing can reduce stress levels and also helps to improve your immune system so that you are better able to fight illnesses.

6 DON'T MOAN

Positive people live longer. If you're an optimist, then you are likely to live 12 years longer than a pessimist. Researchers at the US Mayo Clinic found that pessimists are more likely to get viral illnesses and they are much less likely to check their own physical health. Positive people also have a lower risk of suffering from heart disease and are better able to cope with stress.

SPEAKING

A DISCUSS Work in groups. Discuss the questions.

1 Why do you think so many people continue to do things that are widely known to be harmful to their health?
2 Do you think it is more important to focus on your physical or mental health? Why?
3 What can be done to reduce the risk of obesity, heart disease and other illnesses that are all associated with modern lifestyles?
4 What could be done to increase life expectancy in your country?

B PRESENT Present the main conclusions of your discussion to the rest of the class. Explain your reasoning.

LISTENING

A SPEAK Work in pairs. Look at the pictures (a–f) and discuss the questions.

1 Which of these things would you find difficult to give up? Why?

2 What are some of the potential benefits of giving these things up?

3 What other things do people often try to give up?

4 Have you ever tried to give anything up? How successful were you?

B PREDICT People often decide to give things up at the start of a new year. How successful do you think they are? What percentage of people do you think break their New Year's resolution after:

a a month?   b a year?

C LISTEN FOR GIST Listen to the first part of a radio programme about lifestyle changes and check your predictions from Exercise B.
2.1

D LISTEN FOR MAIN IDEAS Listen to the next part of the radio programme. Match the speakers (1–5) to the things that they have given up from Exercise A. There is one more option than you need.
2.2

Speaker 1 _____

Speaker 2 _____

Speaker 3 _____

Speaker 4 _____

Speaker 5 _____

E LISTEN FOR REASONS Listen to the interviews again. What reason(s) does each speaker give for their lifestyle change? Make notes. Use the information in the box to help you.
2.2

Listening for reasons

In interviews, speakers are often asked to explain their reasons for a particular action or belief. Reasons are usually signalled with:

- **Fixed words and expressions** (e.g. *because (of), as/ since, that's why, due to the fact that, in order to, etc*). *As my family still lives in the area, we decided to move back there.*

- **Infinitives of purpose** *I stopped eating red meat **to help** reduce my blood pressure.*

However, speakers don't always explicitly state their reasons for something. Often, we need to guess the implied meaning from context:

I just remember reading a lot of articles about the impact smoking can have, not only on your health, but on the health of everyone around you. I quit last summer, and I feel much, much healthier.

(= We can guess from the context that the speaker stopped smoking because of the articles they read.)

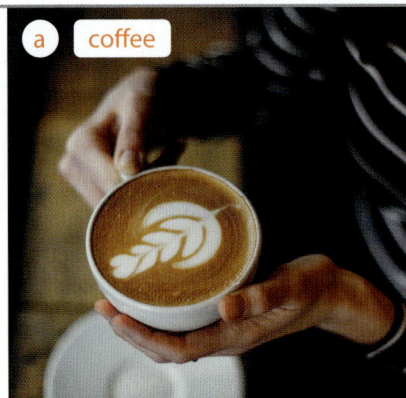
a coffee

b meat

c smartphone

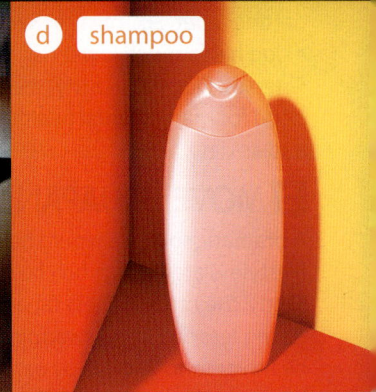
d shampoo

e social media

f sugar

GRAMMAR
Present perfect simple and present perfect continuous

A Work in pairs. Read the extracts from the radio programme and answer the questions.

1 Which sentence describes a finished action? Which describes an unfinished action?

a Yeah, I've actually given up coffee.

b We've been spending more time together as a family.

2 Which sentence focuses on the present effect and which focuses on the action itself?

a I've managed to lose a bit of weight.

b We've been living without smartphones and tablets for six months now.

3 Which sentence is a temporary action and which is permanent?

a My car's in the garage at the moment, so I've been cycling to work for the past two weeks.

b Well, this is going to sound weird, but I've stopped using shampoo.

4 Which sentence focuses on frequency? Which focuses on duration?

a I've only had three chocolate bars this month!

b I've been living without coffee for months now.

B WORK IT OUT Choose the correct options to complete the rules.

Present perfect simple and present perfect continuous

a finished vs unfinished
We use the present perfect [1]*simple / continuous* for finished actions with a present effect, and the present perfect [2]*simple / continuous* for unfinished actions.

b result vs action
We use the present perfect [3]*simple / continuous* to emphasise the result of an action, and the present perfect [4]*simple / continuous* to highlight the action itself.

c temporary vs permanent
We use the present perfect [5]*simple / continuous* to suggest that something is permanent, and the present perfect [6]*simple / continuous* to suggest something is temporary.

d frequency vs duration
We use the present perfect [7]*simple / continuous* to say how much / many times something has happened, and the present perfect [8]*simple / continuous* to say how long something has continued to happen for.

C Go to the Grammar Hub on page VIII.

D PRACTISE Complete the sentences with the present perfect simple or present perfect continuous of the verbs in brackets. If both are possible, use the continuous form.

1 I _____ (stop) working 12 hours a day.

2 She _____ (try) to spend less time on social media but she's finding it hard.

3 I _____ (work) at a restaurant to pay my university fees.

4 I _____ (be) to the gym five times this week.

5 I _____ (exercise) all morning. I can't wait for lunch.

6 I _____ (give up) junk food and now I feel great!

E SPEAK Work in pairs. Use the prompts to ask and answer questions in the present perfect simple or present perfect continuous.

1 How many times / you / check / social media today?

2 What / you / give up / in the last ten years? Why?

3 What / you / do / recently in order to be healthier?

PRONUNCIATION
Connected speech: present perfect continuous

A Listen to three extracts from the radio programme. Is there a pause between the words in bold? Is the strong or weak form of *been* used?
2.3

1 We've **been spending** more time together as a family.

2 Absolutely! I've **been living** without coffee for months now.

3 I've **been cycling** to work for the past two weeks.

B Listen and complete the sentences.
2.4

1 _____ working really hard recently.

2 _____ using my phone too much lately.

3 _____ eating less junk food.

4 _____ spending more time together.

5 _____ going to the gym a lot lately.

C Listen again and repeat the sentences.
2.4

SPEAKING HUB

A PREPARE What have you been doing too much of recently? What have you not been doing enough of recently? Make notes about:

- use of technology
- diet
- exercise
- family

B PLAN Work in pairs. Write six questions you could ask other students about their habits. Use your notes from Exercise A to help you.

1 *What unhealthy foods have you been eating too much of?*

2 *How often have you seen your family this month?*

C SPEAK Ask other students in the class your questions. Try to give each other advice on changes you could make.

A: *How often have you seen your family this month?*

B: *I haven't seen them at all! I'm just so busy all the time.*

A: *Well maybe you could try phoning them once a week? You don't need to talk for long, but it's important to stay in touch.*

○– **Talk about health and lifestyle choices**
○– **Plan and conduct a lifestyle survey**

2.2 Change

○— Conduct an interview about lifestyle changes
○— Debate the impact of smartphones

G— *used to, would, get used to, be used to*   **P**— catenation: *used to*
S— identifying assumptions   **V**— adverbs of stance; adverb + adjective collocations

LISTENING

A SPEAK Work in pairs. You're going to listen to an interview with a family that has moved from the city to a remote island. What do you think would be the advantages and disadvantages of such a move?

B LISTEN FOR GIST Listen to the interview. Which members of the family are happy with the move? Which aren't?

2.5

C LISTEN FOR DETAIL Listen to the interview again. Choose the correct options (a, b or c) to complete the sentences.

2.5

1 Frank made the decision to leave London because …
   a he found his job too demanding.
   b he found his lifestyle uneventful.
   c he couldn't afford to live there.

2 Since moving to the island, the family …
   a largely eats food that is home-grown or caught.
   b has to spend a lot of money at the local shop.
   c generally has a much better diet than before.

3 Frank says that the family's new lifestyle …
   a was surprisingly easy to adapt to.
   b is less physically demanding.
   c has tested them financially.

4 Katie cannot stream media on the island because …
   a the mountains affect her phone signal.
   b the internet connection is terrible.
   c the family cannot afford the internet.

5 Katie is homeschooled by her mother because …
   a there isn't a good school on the island.
   b she is planning to take UK exams.
   c it gives her more time to collect food.

6 Frank thinks his son enjoys life on the island because …
   a there are lots of young children to play with.
   b he's allowed to play outside all day.
   c he hated growing up in London.

D SPEAK Work in pairs. Imagine moving to a small island far away from where you live. What would you miss? What would you be happy to leave behind?

GRAMMAR
used to, would, get used to, be used to

A Work in pairs. Match the extracts from the interview (1–4) to their meaning (a–d).

1 I **used to work** long hours and it was stressful.
2 I'm **used to getting up** at 6 o'clock every day…
3 Financially, it has also been much harder but we're **getting used to it**.
4 Back in London **he'd complain** about his work constantly.

a This situation is still strange, but it's becoming more familiar.
b This habit was true in the past but isn't true now.
c This situation was true in the past but isn't true now.
d This was strange at first but is normal for me now.

B WORK IT OUT Complete the rules with the words in the box.

> be used to   get used to   used to / didn't use to   would

used to, would, get used to, be used to

We use ¹_____ + infinitive to talk about finished habits and states: things that were true in the past but aren't true now.

We can also use ²_____ + infinitive to talk about finished habits and routines, but not to talk about states.

We use ³_____ to talk about something that was unfamiliar but is not unfamiliar now.

We use ⁴_____ to talk about something that is still unfamiliar and not a current habit.

C Go to the **Grammar Hub** on **page VIII**.

D PRACTISE Complete the sentences with *used to, would, be used to* or *get used to* and the verbs in brackets.

1 I _____ (look) very different when I was younger.

2 I _____ (not / like) mornings but now I enjoy getting up early.

3 When I was a teenager, I _____ (eat) a lot of junk food.

4 I _____ (work) long hours now. I've done it for years.

5 I am _____ (cook) for myself but I'm still not great at it.

6 When I was younger, I _____ (play) video games for hours.

7 I _____ (not / drive). I only passed my test recently.

8 I've decided to cut down on sugar. I _____ (eat) less but it's a bit boring!

E PRACTISE Rewrite the sentences in Exercise D so they are true for you.

F SPEAK Work in pairs. Discuss your sentences from Exercise E. Ask follow-up questions for more information.

PRONUNCIATION
Catenation: *used to*

A Listen to these extracts from the interview. Do we pronounce the final /d/ in *used to*? Do we use the strong or weak form of *to*?

2.6

1 I used to dream of living a quieter and more peaceful life.

2 I'm getting used to being isolated from everyone.

3 I guess I'm not used to it yet.

B Listen and repeat the sentences.

2.7

1 She used to have long hair.

2 Have you got used to living on your own?

3 I'm used to getting up early every day.

4 I actually used to drink a lot of coffee.

5 Don't worry, he's used to it by now.

SPEAKING

A PREPARE Think about how your life has changed in the last ten years. Make a list of positive changes in these areas:

- where you live
- family
- work
- education
- free time
- health

B PLAN Make notes about the three biggest changes in Exercise A. Use these questions to help you:

- What prompted the change?
- How has the change affected your life?
- Are you used to the change yet?

C SPEAK Work in groups. Take turns explaining your changes. Ask follow-up questions for more information.

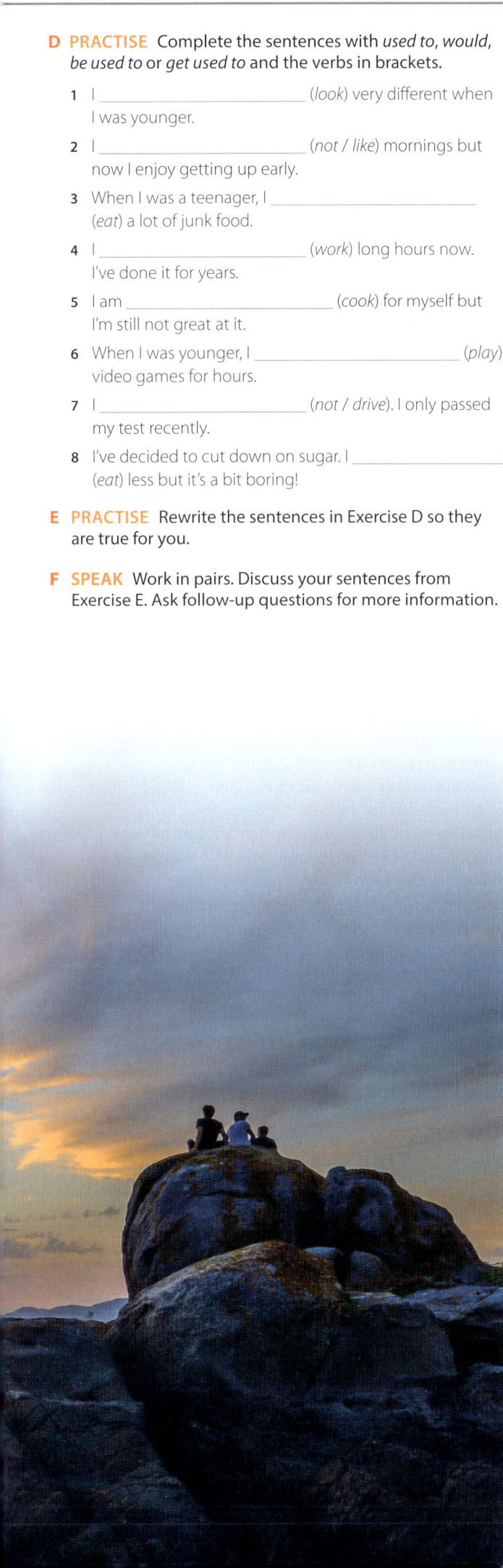

READING

A SPEAK Work in groups. What are some of the positive and negative effects of social media?

B SCAN Read *The big debate* quickly. Which of your ideas from Exercise A are discussed?

C READ FOR GIST Read the article again. Choose the most appropriate debate question (1–4) for the article.

1 Should social media be banned?
2 Have relationships in society got worse?
3 Has social media made us less social?
4 Should we reconnect with the people around us?

THE BIG DEBATE

PETE LOMAS, PSYCHOLOGIST

Admittedly, the internet is pretty much the greatest invention of all time. However, I'd argue that social media is the worst invention to appear in this internet era. It seems to me that despite being 'in contact' with more and more people, we are in fact losing contact – meaningful contact – with most people in our lives.

[a]Beyond question, we're less comfortable in social settings than we once were. **Sadly**, we have all sat around a table where no one is really talking as they skim through their social media. Research by Ofcom has found that 51% of adults and 65% of teenagers have used their smartphone while socialising. **Frankly**, this is going to have a negative impact on our relationships. In fact, in some countries, groups of friends now have a rule – if you check your phone during dinner in a restaurant, then you have to pay for everyone. Are we really in a position where we need to fine people to get them to pay attention to us? [b]Unfortunately, it's not just affecting how we interact but it is also making us feel worse, not better. **Naturally**, constant communication transforms how you feel, especially if you monitor emails, text messages and status updates. There is even an acronym for this phenomenon: FOMO – 'fear of missing out'. [c]As I see it, anything social should make us feel involved but social media is clearly making some people feel left out rather than part of something.

Social media should be renamed anti-social media. [d]In an already isolated world, social media is cutting us off from the world around us even further.

AMY DAY, APP DEVELOPER

From my perspective, social media has **undoubtedly** enhanced our relationships with others. It is true that not all of our online relationships are as close as our face-to-face connections but, on the other hand, it has allowed us to reconnect with lost friends, maintain connections and build new ones.

[e]From my point of view, modern life had already made us all quite isolated individuals. We work long hours. We commute long distances. We move to cities where we know nobody, just for work. Our families all move around, not just in the country we live in, but also to different countries. I'm sure that social media has **simply** emerged from the pressures of modern life and our desire to connect with others despite these obstacles.

Apparently, we are giving up face-to-face relationships with people in favour of less personal social media ones. In all honesty, I don't think this could be further from the truth. According to research by Marketing Charts using data from Nielsen, in the space of five years, TV viewing by 18–24 year olds has fallen from 25 hours a week to **merely** 12. Those aged over 50 still watch over 40 hours a week and this figure isn't declining. Young people are clearly giving up anti-social activities in favour of other ways of interacting.

People who argue that social media has made us less interactive with the world around us clearly have the image in their mind of people on a train with their heads down looking at their phones. These people aren't choosing to be antisocial. [f]Far from it – they are choosing to interact with the people they deem important in their own lives.

D IDENTIFY ASSUMPTIONS Read the article again. Match the sentences in the text (a–f) with the assumptions (1–6). Use the information in the box to help you.

Identifying assumptions

Writers often make assumptions about what groups of people think or the opinions of others. These are signalled with phrases such as *As we all know …*, *Without doubt …* and *Beyond question …*, which are used to try to convince the reader of a certain point of view.

The assumption can also be implied rather than stated directly. For example:

It seems to me that despite being 'in contact' with more and more people, we are in fact losing contact, meaningful contact, with most people in our lives.

(= assumes that online contact is not meaningful.)

1 Previous generations were all good at socialising. _____

2 Nobody that uses social media feels like they're part of a group. _____

3 Social media makes nobody feel positive. _____

4 The world was disconnected before social media. _____

5 Everyone on their phone is using social media. _____

6 Everyone in the modern world felt disconnected anyway. _____

E SPEAK Work in groups. Which of the assumptions in the text do you agree with? Which do you disagree with? Why?

VOCABULARY
Adverbs of stance

A Scan the article again. Complete the definitions with the adverbs in bold.

1 _____ used to say that something is true even though it may weaken your argument

2 _____ based only on what you have heard, not on what you are certain is true

3 _____ used to emphasise that you are about to give your honest opinion, even though the person you are talking to might not like it

4 _____ used to emphasise that something is small or unimportant

5 _____ in the way that you would expect

6 _____ used to say that something is certainly true or is accepted by everyone

7 _____ used to show that you think something is bad or wrong

8 _____ used to emphasise that you are saying something in a plain and straightforward way

B Choose the correct options to complete the sentences.

1 *Naturally / Sadly*, all new developments come with both advantages and disadvantages.

2 *Merely / Admittedly*, I see less of my friends in person now.

3 *Frankly / Apparently*, we have a weaker sense of community than we used to, but I'm not sure I agree.

4 Social media is *merely / apparently* another method of communication.

5 *Simply / Frankly*, I think social media enhances relationships.

6 The internet has *undoubtedly / apparently* enhanced many aspects of our lives. I don't think anyone could question that.

7 I think many people regret the breakdown of communities. *Sadly / Naturally*, many communities are not as close as they once were.

8 It's quite *simply / merely* the best solution to the problem.

VOCABULARY

Adverb + adjective collocations

Some adverbs and adjectives are commonly used together. For example, we say *strongly opposed* NOT ~~deeply opposed~~ or ~~utterly opposed~~. Learning these collocations will help make your language sound more natural.

Complete the sentences with the adverbs in the box.

absolutely   bitterly   deeply   highly   ridiculously

1 It is _____ likely that more and more of our relationships will be conducted using phones.

2 It is _____ ridiculous to say that smartphones have been negative for relationships.

3 I think society should be _____ concerned about the negative impact of smartphones.

4 Smartphones make it _____ easy to stay in touch with people.

5 I was _____ disappointed when my friend started checking her phone during dinner.

⭕ SPEAKING HUB

A PLAN Work in pairs. How do you use technology to support your relationships?

B PREPARE Work in two groups. You are going to debate the following:

Smartphones have had a negative impact on our personal relationships.

Group A – You agree with the statement above.

Group B – You disagree with the statement above.

Plan your arguments. Think about how to support your position, as well as what the other group might say.

C SPEAK Hold a class debate.

◯– **Conduct an interview about lifestyle changes**
◯– **Debate the impact of smartphones**

▶ Ella's story

COMPREHENSION

A Work in groups. Look at the picture and discuss the questions.

1 You are going to watch a video about clean eating. What do you think this term means? Why?

2 Do you pay close attention to your diet? Why/Why not?

3 Who or what influences the food you eat?

> **Glossary**
>
> **gluten (n)** a natural, sticky substance found in some foods (e.g. wheat)
> **vegan (n)** someone who doesn't eat anything made from animals or fish, including eggs, milk and cheese

B ▶ Watch the interview with Ella Mills and answer the questions.

1 Why is Dr Yeo interviewing Ella Mills for the programme?

2 What do all of Ella's recipes have in common?

3 What made Ella decide to change her diet?

4 What did Ella give up as part of her change in diet?

C ▶ Watch the interview again. Are these sentences true (T) or false (F)? Correct the false sentences.

1 Ella's first cookbook wasn't very successful when it was originally published.   *T / F*

2 Ella decided to become a vegetarian more than ten years ago.   *T / F*

3 Ella felt that her original medical treatment wasn't working effectively.   *T / F*

4 Ella was initially doubtful that a change in diet could improve her condition.   *T / F*

5 The fact that many others could identify with her experience encouraged Ella to continue sharing her story online.   *T / F*

D Work in groups. Discuss the questions.

1 As Dr Yeo refers to 'Professor Google' in the video, what do you think his attitude is towards seeking medical advice online?

2 Do you think it's a good idea to search for medical advice online? Why/Why not?

AUTHENTIC ENGLISH

A Work in pairs. Read the extracts from the interview (1–4). Underline the words and phrases used to make the sentences more emphatic.

1 … and her debut cookbook was the fastest-selling ever in the UK.

2 I was the least vegetarian person you would have ever met in your life.

3 … and I came across lots of stories of people who'd used a change in diet and lifestyle to help manage all kinds of conditions, which I was, to be honest, incredibly sceptical of …

4 Her story of how she changed her diet to change her health has proved hugely influential.

B Read the information in the box and check your answers to Exercise A. How else can you make what you say more emphatic?

> **Adding emphasis**
>
> In informal spoken English, speakers often use superlatives, adverbs of degree, *ever/never* and expressions like *in your life* to exaggerate or make their sentences more emphatic. Doing so helps maintain the interest of the listener or highlight the importance of what's being said.

C Work in pairs. Take turns talking about the following topics. Use the techniques in Exercise B to make your descriptions more emphatic.

1 a terrible meal you once had

2 an amazing film you've seen

3 a terrifying experience

The worst meal I've ever had was when I was on holiday in Thailand. I was with my …

▶ You are what you eat

 SAM  MALCOLM  AMANDA  HARRY  EMILY

A Work in pairs. Discuss what you had for breakfast and what you think your partner's choices say about them.

B ▶ Watch the video. What are the differences between Emily and Malcolm's attitudes towards food?

SPEAKING SKILL

A ▶ Watch the video again. Complete the box with examples from the conversation.

Backchannelling and lexical repetition

Backchannelling

Giving signals to show we are interested in what the other speaker is saying is called backchannelling.

To show interest, we say things like *I see* or just make noises like [1] _____, _____.

To show surprise, we say single words like [2] _____, _____, _____.

Lexical repetition

Another way to show we're engaged is lexical repetition. Sometimes this means using the same words as someone else. For example, when Emily first talks about clean eating, Malcolm starts his next turn by saying *clean eating* to show that he is following the topic. Another form of lexical repetition is to rephrase what has been said.

Emily: For me, it's about eating mindfully – I mean, really thinking about what you're putting into your body and how your body uses the energy.

Malcolm: I see. So it's just about trying to eat [3] _____?

Emily: Yeah, making sure your body is getting [4] _____.

B Work in pairs. Student A – Make a comment about one of the topics below. Student B – Rephrase your partner's comment to show you're engaged. Then swap roles.

- the weather today
- a type of food you like
- a film you like
- a country you've been to
- a city you know
- what you are wearing
- a singer or band

A: It's lovely and sunny today.
B: Oh, it's beautiful, isn't it?

SPEAKING HUB

A PREPARE Brainstorm a list of the advantages and disadvantages of becoming a vegan.

B PLAN Do you think you could become a vegan? Why/Why not? Use your ideas from Exercise A to make notes.

C DISCUSS Work in pairs. Discuss whether or not you would be prepared to become a vegan. Explain your reasoning.

A: I don't think I could ever be a vegan. I enjoy eating meat too much.
B: But what about the health benefits? Lots of people believe that vegans have a much longer, healthier life.

◯─ **Give your opinion on food choices**

➤ Turn to page XXV to learn how to write an article giving advice.

VOCABULARY

A Match the causes (1–6) to their effects (a–f) to form full sentences.

1 High-**calorie** diets …
2 Regular **physical** exercise …
3 Strong friendship groups can **reduce the risk of** …
4 A low-calorie diet may **slow the ageing process** …
5 Eating heavily **processed foods** may result in …
6 Maintaining a good **level of fitness** could be positive …

a can result in reduced levels of **stress**.
b **depression** occurring.
c a person's **cholesterol** levels rising.
d could lead to higher levels of **obesity**.
e for a person's **mental health**.
f and lead to a longer **life expectancy**.

B Replace the words in italics with adverbs from the box.

> admittedly   apparently   frankly   merely
> naturally   sadly   simply   undoubtedly

1 I didn't say you had to do it, I *only* suggested you might want to.
2 Have you heard about Mark and Emily? *I'm not sure, but I was told* they're having a baby!
3 That's *just* not true! We sent them multiple emails asking for more time.
4 Tom didn't get the job. *As you'd expect,* he's pretty disappointed, but I'm sure he'll get over it.
5 *It's obvious that* stress has played a large part in her decision.
6 *To be honest,* I think you need to spend more time with your family.
7 *It's true that* I don't do enough exercise.
8 *I'm disappointed that* we can't go on holiday this summer.

C Choose the best adverbs to complete the collocations.

1 I'm *bitterly / deeply* concerned about his mental health at the moment.
2 You should try the 'couch to 5K' running plan. It's *highly / ridiculously* easy.
3 This diet is *absolutely / deeply* dreadful. I don't see how anyone can stick to it.
4 I was *bitterly / absolutely* disappointed when I heard I hadn't got the job.
5 It's *ridiculously / highly* likely that she'll pass the exam and get into the university.
6 It was *bitterly / deeply* cold outside and I'd forgotten my winter coat.
7 Have you ever seen *The shining*? It's *highly / absolutely* terrifying!
8 The actor admitted he was *deeply / ridiculously* ashamed of his behaviour.

GRAMMAR

A Complete the conversations with the present perfect simple or present perfect continuous form of the verbs in the box.

> decorate   have   live   reply   send   travel

1 **A:** We must be nearly there by now – we _____ for hours!
   B: Don't worry, not long to go!
2 **A:** Have you managed to get hold of Andy yet?
   B: No! I _____ him half a dozen emails, but he still _____.
3 **A:** Where are you staying at the moment?
   B: I _____ with my parents while I look for a new flat.
4 **A:** What are you working on?
   B: The same thing! I _____ the same house for weeks now!
5 **A:** Do you want to go for a coffee?
   B: No, I'd better not. I _____ three already this morning.

B Complete the letter with *used to, would, be used to* or *get used to* and the correct form of the verbs in the box.

> arrive   be (x2)   drive   go   know   live   run

Before the internet

In the past, if someone 'followed' you, then you [1]_____ quickly in the opposite direction. 'Going viral' [2]_____ a bad thing and 'trolls' were only toys and not unpleasant people. Arguments [3]_____ on for ages because no one could quickly find the answer on their phone. People [4]_____ everyone's phone numbers off by heart. If you wanted to meet your friends, they [5]_____ on time otherwise it was impossible to find them later. Nowadays, people [6]_____ without a map and never having to plan their journeys. We all seem to have [7]_____ in a world where people speak to their devices as if they're human! I have to say that of all these changes – one thing I'll never [8]_____ is these devices spying on me!

Richard Solomon

Harlow, Essex

C Work in pairs. Discuss the questions.

1 What did you used to look like when you were younger?
2 What's something that you used to hate, but now love?
3 Do you think you're used to speaking in English yet?
4 What would someone have to get used to if they lived in your country?

SURVIVAL

Courage is knowing what not to fear.

Plato

Nearing the summit of the Totem Pole in Tasmania, Australia.

OBJECTIVES

- create a collaborative story
- tell a personal anecdote
- discuss priorities in a survival situation
- talk about fears and offer advice
- describe a journey
- write a short story

Work with a partner. Discuss the questions.

1   Read the quote. What do you think Plato means?

2   Look at the picture. What would you be afraid of if you were alone in this place?

3   What skills and strengths do you have to survive a challenging situation?

3.1 Staying alive

● Create a collaborative story
● Tell a personal anecdote

S – following the sequence of a narrative   G – narrative tenses
V – descriptive verbs   P – dramatic storytelling techniques

READING

A SPEAK Work in pairs. Discuss how you might survive in the following situations.

1 Your plane crashes in the jungle and you're lost without a phone.

2 On a climb in the Alps, you trip and break your ankle.

3 Your boat sinks, but you manage to swim to a desert island.

4 While driving through the Sahara, your jeep breaks down, miles from any towns.

5 There's a fire in your office building and you're on the top floor.

B READ FOR GIST Read *Nigerian cook survives for three days in an underwater air bubble* and answer the questions. Make notes.

1 Who is the main focus of the story?

2 What happened to the Jascon-4?

3 How did the ship's cook survive for three days?

4 What happened to the other crew members?

5 How was the cook eventually rescued?

C FOLLOW THE SEQUENCE OF A NARRATIVE Read the article again. Put the events in the order they happened. Use the information in the box to help you.

Following the sequence of a narrative

Articles describing the sequence of past events don't always present the information in chronological order. To help you identify the order in which things happened, look for:

Time expressions

Writers use a combination of specific time expressions (e.g. *at 5 am, on 26th May*, etc) and phrases (e.g. *24 hours later, over the next three days*, etc) to highlight key points in the narrative.

Tenses

Identifying which tense has been used and why (e.g. past perfect to show that one action happened before another) will also help you to understand when events happened in relation to each other.

___ He woke up and went to the bathroom.

___ He found some equipment.

___ He gave the divers a huge shock.

___ He thought he heard sharks outside.

___ He stopped the water coming in.

___ The boat was turned over by a powerful wave.

___ He opened the door and went into the corridor.

___ He knocked on the wall with a hammer.

___ He spent two days recovering.

Nigerian cook SURVIVES for THREE DAYS in UNDERWATER AIR BUBBLE

Harrison Okene was trapped 30 metres below the surface in freezing waters.

Harrison Okene was a happy young man who was about to get married in a few days. At the time, he was working as a cook on a boat and before getting married, he had to go on one last trip. Unfortunately, it quickly turned into a nightmare.

The events started to unfold at 5.00 am on 26th May. The crew of the Jacson-4 had been sleeping while the boat was resting 20 miles off the Nigerian coast. While a violent storm was raging, Okene got up to go to the toilet. As he was standing in the bathroom, a huge wave hit the boat. It turned over and plunged 30 metres below the surface, with Okene and the rest of the crew still inside. Water quickly began to fill the cabin, blocking the toilet door as the boat sank into the sea. Using all his strength, Okene forced open the door and headed out into the corridor. Wearing nothing but pyjamas, he waded through the corridor in total darkness towards the only light he could see. Quickly he grabbed a drink and a few tools and made it to the light.

Stuck in a small pocket of air, he blocked the sides with furniture to keep the water out. Unknown to Okene, all of his crewmates had already drowned. With hardly any air to breathe, time was running out. Hungry, cold and tired, Okene thought he could hear sharks circling the boat and started to lose hope. However, his luck was about to change.

When a rescue crew arrived, they assumed everyone had died as the boat had been resting on the seabed for 60 hours. Realising the sounds he had heard were human, Okene started banging on the wall with a hammer. Thinking he wouldn't be discovered, he jumped into the water and began swimming through the ship. Seeing a rescue diver swim past him, Okene reached out to touch the man on the shoulder. Although initially terrified, the diver realised he'd found a survivor and called for support. Shortly afterwards, Okene was strapped to diving equipment and taken back to the surface where he spent two days in a decompression chamber.

GRAMMAR
Narrative tenses

A Complete the sentences with the correct form of the verbs in brackets. Then scan the article again to check your answers.

1 At the time, he _____ (work) as a cook on a boat.

2 While a violent storm _____ (rage) outside, Okene got up to go to the toilet.

3 It _____ (turn) over and plunged 30 metres below the surface, with Okene and the rest of the crew still inside.

4 Unknown to Okene, all of his shipmates _____ _____ (already / drown).

5 When a rescue crew arrived, they assumed everyone had died, as the boat _____ (rest) on the seabed for 60 hours.

B **WORK IT OUT** Choose the correct tenses to complete the rules in the box.

> #### Narrative tenses
>
> We use the ¹*past simple / past perfect* for completed actions that are the main events in a story.
>
> We use the ²*past continuous / past simple*:
> - for actions in progress at a particular point in time.
> - when a longer action is interrupted by a shorter action.
> - to set the scene of a story.
>
> We use the ³*past perfect / past perfect continuous* for completed actions that happened before the main event.
>
> We use the ⁴*past perfect / past perfect continuous* for longer actions that started before other events and continued up to these events.

C Go to the Grammar Hub on page X.

D **PRACTISE** Complete the text with the correct form of the verbs in brackets.

NEWS SPORT CULTURE LIFESTYLE   SEARCH 🔍

7-YEAR-OLD JAPANESE BOY SURVIVES FOR OVER A WEEK ALONE IN THE WOODS

FAMILY DAY OUT TURNS TO DISASTER

A family day out looking for wild vegetables quickly turned to disaster when a boy's parents decided to punish his bad behaviour. Yamato Tanooka ¹_____ (throw) stones at cars as he waited for his parents. Spotting his behaviour, his father quickly ²_____ (become) very angry and ³_____ (shout) at him. To punish their son, Mr and Mrs Tanooka ⁴_____ (leave) him on the side of the road and ⁵_____ (drive) a few hundred metres away. By the time they ⁶_____ (drive) back to the spot, Yamato ⁷_____ (already / leave). His father ⁸_____ (phone) the police and ⁹_____ (say) he ¹⁰_____ (become) separated from his son while they ¹¹_____ (pick) wild vegetables. In the meantime, Yamato ¹²_____ (walk) off into the woods, upset that his father ¹³_____ him _____ (tell off). When the army finally ¹⁴_____ (find) Yamato, he ¹⁵_____ (live) for six days on his own in woods that are home to brown bears. Yamato told reporters that he ¹⁶_____ (walk) for five hours through the woods when he found an old army cabin. Afraid of the dark, he decided to hide there and wait for his parents to find him.

E **PRACTISE** Work in groups. Write the first sentence of a dramatic story. Pass your sentence to the student on your right. Add another sentence to the story you have just received. Keep doing this until your story is complete.

SPEAKING

A **PREPARE** Go to the Communication Hub on page XX.

B **PRESENT** Choose one person to tell your story to the class. Listen to the other stories and ask questions about the details.

LISTENING

A Label the pictures (1–6) with the activities in the box.

> bungee jumping   free running   free climbing
> potholing   skydiving   whitewater rafting

B SPEAK Work in pairs. Discuss the questions.

1 Which of these sports do you think is the most dangerous? Why?

2 Why do you think some people enjoy doing dangerous sports like these?

3 Have you ever done any of these sports? Would you like to? Why/Why not?

C LISTEN FOR GIST Listen to a radio talk show about extreme sports and answer the questions. Make notes.

3.1

1 Which of the sports from Exercise A do the speakers talk about?

2 How many of the speakers have has been injured whilst doing their sport?

D LISTEN FOR DETAIL Listen again and choose the correct options (a, b or c) to complete the sentences.

3.1

1 Paul started free climbing when he was …
  a 10 years old.   b 17 years old.   c 27 years old.

2 Paul thinks climbing without safety equipment …
  a is a terrible idea.
  b is a good challenge.
  c allows him to go higher.

3 Paul was most scared when …
  a he was caught in strong winds during a climb.
  b the bridge he was crossing on broke.
  c a snake shot out of a crack in a rock.

4 Hayley thinks that …
  a potholing is more challenging than rock climbing.
  b rock climbing is too challenging.
  c potholing is more like walking than climbing.

5 Hayley was lost underground for …
  a a few minutes.   b a few hours.   c a few days.

6 Lee started free running …
  a because his friends were doing it.
  b because he saw a film of people doing it.
  c because he wanted something more challenging than gymnastics.

7 Lee most enjoys …
  a the physical challenge of free running.
  b the way free running makes you look at a city.
  c the risks involved in free running.

8 Lee says that …
  a you should push yourself beyond your limits.
  b you need to be very competitive to be good at free running.
  c you should only do what you know you are capable of.

E SPEAK Work in groups. Discuss the questions.

1 Who do you think had the most frightening experience. Why?

2 Which of the sports would you like to try? Why?

1 _____

2 _____

3 _____

4 _____

VOCABULARY
Descriptive verbs

A Work in pairs. For each extract, choose the option that makes the same sound as the verb in bold.

1 I can still remember the snow **crunching** under our feet as we walked together.
   a old leaves under your feet
   b your feet in an empty hospital corridor

2 Sometimes the wood **groans** under your weight, which can be a bit scary, but so far none have ever actually broken!
   a grass under your feet
   b floorboards under your feet

3 I am terrified of snakes, so I just froze as it started to **hiss** and arch backwards.
   a the wind closing a door
   b air slowly escaping from a tyre

4 It can be silent for just a few minutes and all you can hear is water **trickling** around you.
   a a slow-running tap
   b a large, powerful river

5 I can still hear my ankle **snap** as I landed.
   a a branch breaking
   b a window breaking

B Complete the sentences with the correct form of the verbs in Exercise A.

1 The snake _____ and slithered back into the undergrowth.

2 The leaves were _____ under our feet as we crept slowly through the forest.

3 I could hear the branch of the tree _____ under my weight before it _____ and I fell to the ground.

4 Every time it rained, I could hear water _____ down the wall behind my bed.

C Go to the Vocabulary Hub on **page XVIII**.

D SPEAK Work in pairs. Use descriptive verbs to make this story more interesting.

I was walking through the forest with fallen leaves under my feet. The trees were blowing in the wind. Suddenly, I heard a branch break behind me. I turned to see a huge dog running towards me.

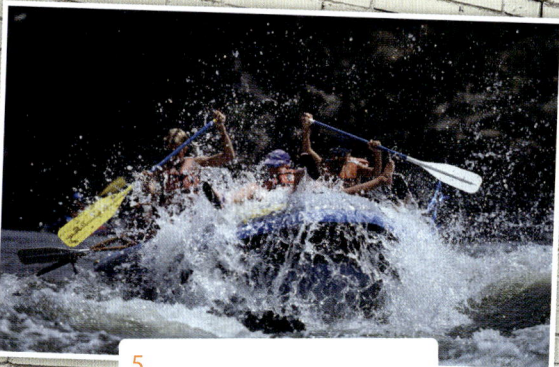

PRONUNCIATION
Dramatic storytelling techniques

A Listen to this extract from the talk show. Mark the pauses with (/) and underline any words that are emphasised.

Well, a few years ago I was in South Africa with a few of my friends and we'd nearly finished the first part of an all-day climb. I was just pulling myself up when I saw a huge snake right in front of me. I am terrified of snakes, so I just froze as it started to hiss and arch backwards. I waited for another few minutes, not moving, and then it just seemed to get bored and slithered back into a crack in the rock. It was the most terrifying moment ever and it had nothing to do with climbing!

B Listen to the story again. When does the speaker speed up and slow down? Why do you think he does this?

C Read the story extract. Predict where you think the pauses will be, which words the speaker will stress and when they will speed up.

So a few months ago I was staying at my parents' house when this strange thing happened. We were all enjoying the warmth of the crackling fire as the trees creaked in the wind outside. Suddenly, we heard glass smashing upstairs and something heavy banged on the floor. We rushed upstairs to find that a huge branch had crashed through the roof of the house.

D Listen and check your answers to Exercise C. Then, practise telling the story with a partner.

◯ SPEAKING HUB

A PLAN Think of the most amazing, terrifying or embarrassing moment in your life. Make notes about:
- where you were
- who you were with
- what happened

B PREPARE Work in pairs. Tell your stories and work together to make them more dramatic or exciting.

C PRESENT Work in small groups. Tell your stories as dramatically as you can. Ask questions to get more information.

6 _____

◯ Create a collaborative story
◯ Tell a personal anecdote

5 _____

● Discuss priorities in a survival situation
● Talk about fears and offer advice

G – alternatives to *if* in conditionals
S – listening for definitions, examples and explanations
P – intonation in conditional sentences
V – phrasal verbs to describe problems; dependent prepositions: adjectives

READING

A SPEAK Work in groups. Discuss what you would do in the following situations.

1 You're caught in some quicksand in the desert. As you're sinking you see a large stick nearby.

2 You're attacked by a swarm of killer bees in the woods. There's a house in the distance and a lake a few metres away.

3 You're doing parachute jump, but your parachute fails. If you stretch out, you could probably reach your friend.

B READ FOR GIST Complete the interview with the questions (a–d).

a Is that in your show this time?

b Can we expect any dangerous animals this year?

c Are you feeling excited about your new series starting next week?

d What can viewers expect from this series?

C READ FOR DETAIL Read again. Choose the correct options (a or b) to complete the sentences.

1 Chuck advises carrying a stick in the desert …
  a to move quicksand away from your body.
  b to stop yourself sinking into quicksand.

2 When you are in quicksand, Chuck suggests …
  a moving quickly to escape.
  b getting out carefully.

3 Chuck says that hitting killer bees …
  a is the first form of defence against them.
  b is likely to make the situation worse.

4 If you follow his advice, Chuck says you may break your arm when …
  a your friend's parachute opens.
  b your parachute opens.

D SPEAK Work in groups. Has anyone you know ever been in a life-threatening situation? How did they survive?

CHUCK ADAMS:

SURVIVE THE WILD

In the office of *Live, Play, Work Magazine,* we're all very excited to see the return to TV of Chuck Adams and his series *Survive the Wild.* Tom Wood caught up with Chuck to ask him about surviving in the desert, killer bees and why breaking your arm is sometimes the best thing to do …

Tom: It's great to see you again, Chuck! [1]___

Chuck: I am. The first series was incredibly popular and we're taking viewers into some even more exciting situations in the new series.

Tom: [2]___

Chuck: Well, we look at how to survive dangerous situations in different locations. From mountains to deserts to the Arctic. For example, in the desert or along the coast, always carry a stick in case you need it. Quicksand is really dangerous! As soon as you start to sink, put the stick on the surface of the sand and lie on it. If you do this, it will stop you sinking. Once you stop sinking, you need to crawl, climb and almost swim out. You'll be OK as long as you move slowly out of the sand. If you move too quickly, you'll sink.

Tom: Sounds like hard work! Last series you looked at surviving crocodile attacks and shark attacks. [3]___

Chuck: Definitely! We have all sorts, including killer bees! People often freeze when they see a bee, but this won't stop it stinging you. And definitely don't try to hit them – this just makes them angrier. If bees fly around you, try to find shelter as quickly as possible. Provided you can get into a building, or shelter in long grass, you'll be fine. Lots of people jump into water to get away. Don't do this. The bees will just be waiting for you when you come up!

Tom: That sounds horrible! What about surviving accidents? [4]___

Chuck: Of course! People usually do parachute jumps with other people. If your parachute doesn't open, grab the person near you, lock your arms together and hold onto each other. When your friend opens their parachute you will survive, but you will also probably break your arm – so be prepared for a bit of pain!

Tom: I feel a bit sick at the thought of breaking my arm!

Chuck: Maybe, but unless you lock arms, you won't survive!

Tom: Well we can't wait for the show to return next week! Thanks for speaking to us today.

GRAMMAR
Alternatives to *if* in conditionals

A Work in pairs. Read the extracts from the interview and choose the correct meaning.

1 … in the desert or along the coast, always carry a stick in case you need it.
   a Take a stick because you will definitely need it.
   b Take a stick because you might need it.

2 As soon as you start to sink, put the stick on the surface of the sand and lie on it.
   a When you start sinking, use the stick immediately.
   b When you start sinking, use the stick when you can.

3 You'll be OK as long as you move slowly out of the sand.
   a It's the only way to get out of the sand.
   b It's one way to get out of the sand.

4 Provided you can get into a building, or shelter in long grass, you'll be fine.
   a You will only be fine if you get into a building or shelter in long grass.
   b You will be fine whatever happens.

5 Maybe, but unless you lock arms, you won't survive!
   a Don't do this and you might survive.
   b Do this or you won't survive.

B **WORK IT OUT** Complete the rules with words and phrases in the box.

as long as   as soon as   in case   provided (that)   unless

Alternatives to *if* in conditionals

We use ¹_____ to mean *if … not*.
We use ²_____ and ³_____ to mean *only if*.
We use ⁴_____ to talk about doing something now to prepare for a possible situation.
We use ⁵_____ to mean in the shortest time possible.

C Go to the Grammar Hub on page X.

D **SPEAK** Work in pairs. Give advice about the following situations using conditional conjunctions.

1 You're in the middle of a field when a thunderstorm begins.
2 You're swimming in the sea when you see a shark swim by.
3 You're lost in the countryside when your phone runs out of battery.
4 You're driving along when your car runs out of petrol.

As long as you can walk to a petrol station, you'll be able to buy petrol.

PRONUNCIATION
Intonation in conditional sentences

A Listen to the conditional sentences. Draw arrows to mark rising (↗) or falling (↘) intonation.
3.4
1 Provided you don't run (__), the bull won't chase you (__).
2 Take a torch (__) in case it gets dark (__).
3 Unless you find a water source (__), you won't survive (__).

B Listen again and repeat the sentences.
3.4

SPEAKING

A **PREPARE** Read the scenario. Make a list of survival priorities.

You are on a small plane that has crashed on a river in a jungle. You can swim to the side of the river, but you can only take a few things with you before the plane sinks. As far as you know, you're a long way from the nearest town and may have to spend a few nights in the jungle.

1 Make a shelter
2 …

B **PLAN** You have found the items below in the plane. Make notes on how you could use each item to help you achieve your priorities from Exercise A.

C **DISCUSS** Work in groups. Together you must decide on three survival priorities and how you will use the items from Exercise B.

A: I think we should use the rope to make a shelter.
B: That's fine by me, as long as we can save some of the rope for fishing.

LISTENING

A SPEAK Work in pairs. Look at the pictures and discuss the questions.

1 What fears are shown in the pictures?

2 Do you think these fears are rational (i.e. based on facts, not emotion) or irrational? Why?

3 What other common fears can you think of?

B LISTEN FOR GIST Listen to an extract from an audiobook about fear. Put the topics in the order they are discussed.

3.5

___ the influence of memory

___ potential dangers of the modern world

___ the physical effects of fear

___ how we assess a perceived threat

___ the brain's initial response

C LISTEN FOR DEFINITIONS, EXAMPLES AND EXPLANATIONS Listen to the extract again. Complete the notes below with no more than three words or a number. Use the information in the box to help you.

3.5

Listening for definitions, examples and explanations

Speakers often use the following to make their ideas clearer:

Definitions

To explain topic-specific language, speakers often provide definitions. These are usually clearly signalled by phrases such as *This is defined as …*, *This means …*, but can also be given mid-sentence (e.g. *Claustrophobia – a fear of being in a small or crowded place – is often …*).

Examples

To help clarify an idea, speakers use examples. These are signalled by phrases such as *For instance …*, *Such as …*, *An example of this is …*

Explanations

To make something easier to understand, speakers may also give explanations. These can be signalled by phrases such as *In other words …*, *That's to say …*, *Let me explain …*

Natural reactions

The amygdala is the section ¹_____ associated with our emotional responses.

²_____ is the body's natural response to a perceived threat.

The hippocampus and the prefrontal cortex help us to distinguish between a ³_____ and a perceived threat. Our ⁴_____ influence this decision.

We often focus on dramatic or emotional events (e.g. although skin cancer causes over ⁵_____ deaths a year, people worry more about plane crashes).

Increased stress and anxiety can have a ⁶_____ on our immune system > could lead to physical and mental health issues. Issue of the modern world?

D SPEAK Work in pairs. Discuss the questions.

1 Do you think the 'fight or flight' response is useful in the modern world? Why/Why not?

2 Why do you think people often refuse to change their mind about something even when shown evidence against it?

3 What kinds of things do people fear now that they didn't fear 20 years ago?

VOCABULARY
Phrasal verbs to describe problems

A Match the phrasal verbs (1–7) to their definitions (a–g).

1 go through   5 deal with

2 sort out   6 work out

3 put up with   7 weigh up

4 talk over

a do what is necessary to solve a problem

b accept someone or something unpleasant in a patient way

c accept and control a difficult emotional situation so that you can start to live a normal life again despite it

d experience something difficult or unpleasant

e solve a problem by considering the facts

f discuss a problem or a plan

g consider the good and bad aspects of something in order to reach a decision about it

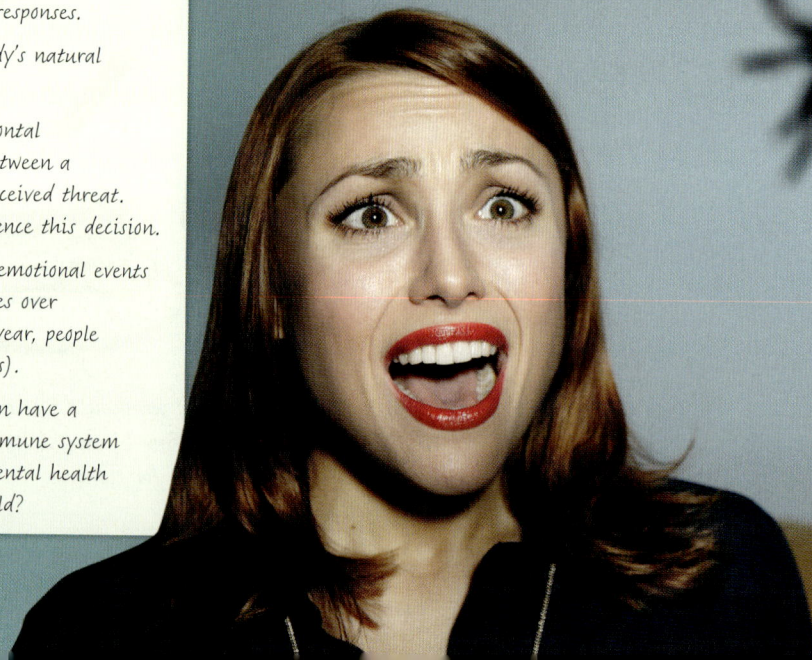

B Choose the correct verbs to complete the questions.

1 Do you think you are good at *working out* / *dealing with* how to solve problems?

2 Do you *talk over* / *deal with* your plans with the people around you?

3 What could you *put up with* / *sort out* more easily – a room full of spiders or snakes?

4 When was the last time you *weighed up* / *put up with* the risks and benefits before making a decision?

5 What scary situation have you recently had to *go through* / *weigh up*? What happened?

6 How would you *sort out* / *weigh up* a situation where everyone was panicking?

7 In general, how well do you *deal with* / *go through* risky situations?

C SPEAK Work in pairs. Discuss the questions in Exercise B.

VOCABULARY
Dependent prepositions: adjectives

Dependent prepositions: adjectives
Some adjectives are usually followed by specific prepositions. These are called 'dependent prepositions' and they are followed by either a noun or *-ing*. For example: *My mother has always been terrified of spiders.* NOT ~~My mother has always been terrified about spiders.~~

Choose the correct prepositions to complete the sentences.

1 I'm really anxious *about* / *to* speaking in public.

2 I feel a bit ashamed *of* / *for* my fear of flying. I know it's not rational.

3 I'm sick *about* / *of* feeling this way – I really need to get some help.

4 I'm envious *for* / *of* people who can stay calm in dangerous situations.

5 They became suddenly aware *of* / *from* the danger around them.

6 I'm not really scared of anything, but I try to be sensitive *towards* / *for* people with a lot of phobias.

SPEAKING HUB

A PREPARE Read the scenarios (1–3). Make notes about what each person is afraid of and how it affects their life.

1 Emily Ronson is a 26-year-old graphic designer working in London. She gets the tube to work every day but hates every minute of the 40-minute journey. Being in tight spaces with lots of people makes her feel incredibly anxious. Sometimes, she feels so overwhelmed that she gets off the train and waits until it's less busy. Sometimes, this makes her late for work. She's ashamed of her fear so she hasn't told anyone about it.

2 Helen Masters is a retired police officer from Manchester. Several times over the past decade, she has had to cancel holidays because she had a panic attack shortly after boarding the plane and demanded to get off. She knows this is an issue but has decided to live with it. Now she rarely travels abroad and cannot see her grandchildren as they live in the USA.

3 Tom Hawksby is a 43-year-old accountant at a large computer software company in New York. Recently, the company haven't been doing well and hundreds of people have lost their jobs. Tom is worried that he'll lose his job, too, and finds it difficult to sleep at night. This is making him tired and angry at work.

B DISCUSS Work in groups. Use your notes from Exercise A to discuss the questions.

1 Which of the fears do you think are irrational? Which are rational? Why?

2 How well do you think each person copes with their fear?

3 Do you think their fear is a big issue? Why/Why not?

4 What would you do in their position?

C PRESENT Choose one person from your group to present the main points of your discussion to the rest of the class.

○– **Discuss priorities in a survival situation**
○– **Talk about fears and offer advice**

▶ The great tepui challenge

COMPREHENSION

A Work in groups. You are going to watch a video of people climbing Amaurai Tepui, a mountain in Venezuela. What do you think are the biggest challenges they will face?

B ▶ Watch the video. What makes the climbers think about giving up?

C ▶ Watch the video again. Are these sentences true (T) or false (F)? Correct the false sentences.

1 The team start day five of the climb near the summit of the mountain.   T / F

2 Presenter, Steve Backshall, hopes the improved weather indicates the end of the storm season.   T / F

3 The team is attempting to become the first to climb this part of the mountain.   T / F

4 One indication of the coming storm is the mass movement of birds.   T / F

5 The team survive the storm by climbing back down the mountain.   T / F

6 Steve thinks it would be a shame to give up having come so far.   T / F

D ▶ Work in pairs. Read the extracts from the video. What do the words in bold refer to? Watch the video again to check your answers.

1 **It** would be nice after yesterday, wouldn't it?

2 There's a big storm coming and **they** know it.

3 **It** left us clinging to the cliff.

4 We've got to get off **this thing**; someone's going die.

5 … nothing is worth risking **this** for.

E Work in groups. Discuss the questions.

1 What do you think Steve means when he says, 'You could taste the fear'?

2 Would you like to take part in such an extreme challenge? Why/Why not?

AUTHENTIC ENGLISH

A Work in pairs. Read the extract from the video. What do you think *fingers crossed* means?

Steve: What do you reckon? Do you think our luck's changing?

Cameraman: Fingers crossed. It would be nice after yesterday, wouldn't it?

B *Fingers crossed* is actually part of a longer idiom. Which of the following do you think completes it?

a Have your …   b Keep your …   c Make your …

C Work in groups. Read the information in the box and guess the meaning of the shortened idioms in bold.

Shortened idioms

Some idioms are so common in informal spoken English that speakers don't need to say them in full for listeners to understand them.

*I've always been unhappy there but having my pay cut was **the last straw** [that broke the camel's back].*

*He called you a liar? Well, **if the shoe fits** [wear it].*

*I'm not surprised Max had a party while we were away. You know what they say – **when the cat's away** [the mice will play].*

*I was just thinking that, too. **Great minds** [think alike].*

D Work in pairs. Take turns reading the sentences and responding with an appropriate shortened idiom.

1 Why does my boss keep saying I'm lazy?

2 Nobody was doing any work when I got back.

3 Apparently we both bought him the same leaving gift.

4 Well, I worked pretty hard so hopefully I'll pass.

5 So, what made you fire her in the end?

▶ Snake Mountain

A Work in pairs. Why do you think people take part in extreme challenges (e.g. climbing mountains, sailing great distances, etc)?

B ▶ Watch the video. Make notes about Malcolm's story (e.g. where it happened, who he was with, etc).

C Work in pairs. Summarise Malcolm's story. Use your notes from Exercise B to help you.

SPEAKING SKILL

A ▶ Watch the video again and complete the extracts.

Sam: And I bet having all those snakes around doesn't make it any easier.

Malcolm: Eh? Snakes?

Sam: ¹_____, if it's called 'Snake Mountain', I assume there are lots of snakes.

Malcolm: … we needed an adventure before we started trying to make our way in the world. Well, ²_____, we were looking for an excuse to postpone looking for a job.

Malcolm: None of us knew what we were doing! Well, ³_____, Peter was a pretty good climber, but the rest of us, well …

Malcolm: We couldn't see a thing. Well, ⁴_____, but visibility was down to about a metre.

Malcolm: So we just carried on all the way to the summit. Though, ⁵_____, I wasn't really thinking straight at the time!

B Work in pairs. What is the function of the phrases you wrote in Exercise A?

C Read the information in the box to check your answers to Exercise B.

Backtracking

Sometimes in conversation we need to correct a mistake in something we've said. This is called backtracking. To do this, we use phrases such as:

What I mean is … / What I meant was …, That is to say …, What I should say is … / What I should have said was …, That's not quite true …, When I say … I really mean …

D Work in pairs. Student A – Talk about your journey to work, school or university today in great detail. When necessary, rephrase what you said to make your description clearer. Student B – Listen and ask questions, forcing Student A to backtrack. Then swap roles.

SPEAKING HUB

A PREPARE Brainstorm a list of interesting, dangerous or exciting journeys you have been on.

B PLAN Choose one of the journeys from Exercise A. Make notes about the following:

- Where were you and why?
- When did this happen?
- Who were you with?
- What were the key events?
- How did you feel before, during and after?

C SPEAK Work in groups. Take turns telling your stories. Listen and ask questions where appropriate. Reformulate and backtrack if you need to.

A: So I was all alone on the boat and I could see a storm coming. I kept saying to myself, 'Fingers crossed I don't sink.'

B: Weren't you scared?

A: Well yeah, to be honest, I was terrified. But it was still an amazing moment.

D REFLECT Whose story was the most exciting? Was it the story itself or the way it was told that made it so exciting?

◯─ Describe a journey

➤ Turn to page XXVI to learn how to write a short story.

VOCABULARY

A Choose the correct options (a, b or c) to complete sentences.

1 All I could hear was water ___ down the rock face.
   a crunching   b trickling   c hissing

2 As he leant forward, the branch ___, sending him falling towards the ground.
   a snapped   b rumbled   c crunched

3 The old wooden bridge ___ under the weight of all of the cars.
   a snapped   b groaned   c growled

4 Suddenly, a young child walked into the road. Slamming on the brakes, the car ___ to a halt.
   a screeched   b crunched   c slammed

5 The gravel ___ under the car's tyres as it slowly pulled away.
   a hissed   b snapped   c crunched

6 In a rage, she stormed out of the room and ___ the door.
   a smashed   b creaked   c slammed

B Complete the second sentence so it has a similar meaning to the first, using the words in bold.

1 It was a terrible experience for them to endure.
   go through
   They had to _____.

2 Someone needs to organise the details of the party.
   sort out
   They need to _____.

3 Try not to get so stressed at work.
   stay calm
   Try _____.

4 I can't quit my job until I find a new one.
   put up with
   I'll have to _____.

5 The management team are discussing the issues together before they make a decision.
   talk over
   Before making a decision, _____.

6 The government must do something about the high level of unemployment.
   deal with
   The government _____.

7 What's wrong with my computer?
   work out
   Can you _____.

8 Let's look at the options and decide which one is best.
   weigh up
   To decide _____.

C Complete the collocations with the adjectives in the box.

anxious   ashamed   aware   envious   sensitive   sick

1 You should be _____ of your behaviour! It's embarrassing!

2 I'm _____ of having to clean up after you all the time.

3 I'm feeling a little _____ about the job interview next week.

4 I think she's _____ of your results – you're always top of the class.

5 Maybe you just need to be more _____ towards other people's feelings.

6 You need to be more _____ of how your actions affect the people around you.

GRAMMAR

A Choose the correct options to complete the sentences.

1 They *left / were leaving* the house and *walked / were walking* to the station.

2 I *felt / was feeling* pretty nervous until we *scored / were scoring* the second goal.

3 I *hadn't taken / hadn't been taking* my mobile phone, so I *had / was having* no way of contacting them.

4 By the time I *had got / got* to the cinema the film *started / had already started*.

5 *I'd been waiting / I'd waited* in the queue for 40 minutes before someone *had served / served* me.

6 I *packed / was packing* my suitcase when the phone *rang / had rung*.

7 I *was working / worked* at my desk when a bird *flew / was flying* into the window.

8 He was exhausted because he *had worked / had been working* all night. He *hadn't slept / hadn't been sleeping* for 24 hours.

B Complete the sentences with *as long as, as soon as, in case, provided (that)* or *unless*. Sometimes more than one option is possible.

1 Call me _____ you hear from him!

2 Don't disturb me _____ it's really urgent.

3 You should bring a snack _____ you get hungry.

4 _____ you work hard, you'll get a pay rise this year.

5 I'm going to buy extra food _____ more people come to the party.

6 _____ you finish the swimming section, you need to get straight onto your bike.

7 I won't accept a contact request on LinkedIn _____ I know them already.

8 It looks like we should get there on time _____ the traffic isn't too bad.

THE FUTURE

The future belongs to those who believe in the beauty of dreams.

Eleanor Roosevelt

A father and daughter programming a VR simulator.

OBJECTIVES

- talk about future plans and goals
- make predictions about the future of work
- evaluate future predictions
- debate a range of transport proposals
- give your opinion on automation in the workplace
- write a for and against blog post

Work with a partner. Discuss the questions.

1 Read the quote. What do you think Roosevelt means? Do you agree with her? Why/Why not?

2 What technological developments do you think will change the world in the future?

3 Are you generally optimistic or pessimistic about the future of the world? Why?

4.1 My future
● Talk about future plans and goals
● Make predictions about the future of work

G – future forms V – noun + preposition collocations; nouns and verbs with the same spelling
S – identifying evidence P – nouns and verbs with the same spelling

LISTENING

A Look at the pictures (a–e). Rank these life decisions from most to least important.

B SPEAK Work in pairs. Compare your ideas from Exercise A. Explain your reasoning. What do you agree about? What do you disagree about?

C LISTEN FOR GIST Listen to a podcast about turning points in people's lives. Match the speakers to the change they talk about.
4.1

1 Lucy   a   planning how to spend their retirement
2 Hadiyah   b   packing in preparation for a gap year abroad
3 Frank   c   getting organised for a new arrival

D LISTEN FOR DETAIL Listen to the podcast again. Choose the correct option (a, b or c) to complete the sentences.
4.1

1 Lucy is planning to …
   a take a course in Spain   c work in the USA
   b drive across Russia

2 Which country isn't Lucy going to?
   a Russia   c Brazil
   b China

3 Hadiyah's husband …
   a thinks they are having a boy.   c is happy with a boy or a girl.
   b thinks they are having a girl.

4 Who in Hadiyah's family are they thinking of naming the baby after?
   a one of the grandmothers   c one of her sisters
   b one of the aunts

5 Frank has just bought …
   a a new car.   c a fishing rod.
   b a new caravan.

6 Frank is planning to …
   a go on a cruise.   c take a road trip.
   b retire in Florida.

E LISTEN FOR KEY INFORMATION Listen again. Use the table to make notes about each speaker
4.1

	Lucy	Hadiyah	Frank
What is each speaker excited about?			
What hasn't each speaker decided?			
What new skill does each speaker talk about?			

F IDENTIFY ASSUMPTIONS Work in groups. Read the extracts (1–2). Do you agree with the assumptions each speaker makes? Why/Why not?

1 Everyone there speaks some English, anyway.
2 Everyone wants to retire, don't they?

a   whether to have a family

b   what to wear

c   where to live

d   what job to do

GRAMMAR
Future forms

A Listen and complete the extracts with the correct future form of the verbs in brackets.

4.2

1 I _____ (fly) to Paris as I have a friend there.

2 The lessons _____ (be) three days a week from nine to four.

3 Then, I _____ (visit) as many countries as I can.

4 Parents are always really busy, so I _____ _____ (definitely / have) to get better at managing my time.

5 Do you think you _____ (miss) work?

6 That's a good idea. I _____ (add) it to the list!

B **WORK IT OUT** Choose the correct tenses to complete the rules.

Future forms

We use the ¹*present simple / present continuous* for definite future arrangements.

We use ²*going to / will* + infinitive to talk about general intentions.

We use ³ *going to / will* + infinitive for decisions made at the moment of speaking.

We use ⁴*present simple / present continuous* for timetabled events.

We use ⁵*will + infinitive / present continuous* for making predictions.

We use ⁶*will / going to* + infinitive for predictions based on something we know.

C Go to the **Grammar Hub** on **page XII**.

D **PRACTISE** Complete the sentences with the correct form of the verbs in the box.

break   come   fly   go   leave   miss   see   text

1 There's no milk left? OK, I _____ Bea and ask her to pick some up.

2 That chair doesn't look very strong – I think it _____!

3 We _____ with Easy Jet on the way out, but haven't booked the return flight yet.

4 The next train to Cambridge _____ at 17.12.

5 She probably _____ – she doesn't really like parties.

6 After uni, I _____ travelling for a year. Not sure where though.

7 We're still miles away from the airport – we _____ our flight!

8 I _____ her on Friday, actually. We've got a meeting at 2 pm.

VOCABULARY
Noun + preposition collocations

Noun + preposition collocations

Some nouns and prepositions are commonly used together. For example, we can say *the reason for* but not *the reason of*.

Correct the prepositions in each sentence.

1 Congratulations for passing the exam!

2 I'm hoping to take a course for accounting.

3 I need to make more time of my family.

4 We're planning to visit lots of places of Europe.

5 There's the possibility to changing jobs next summer.

6 I'm a bit worried. There's the risk for not getting into college.

SPEAKING

A **PREPARE** You are going to interview your partner about their plans and goals for the future. Write questions about:

- home
- study
- work
- family
- travel
- achievements

1 *What are you going to do after your course finishes?*

2 *Would you like to go travelling?*

B **SPEAK** Interview your partner. Ask follow-up questions to find out more information.

A: *When does your course finish?*

B: *At the end of July.*

A: *So, what are you going to do afterwards?*

B: *Hmm … I'm not sure. I'll probably try and find a job in a café or something.*

e   whether to get married

READING

A SPEAK Work in groups. Which jobs do you think will be most affected by robots in the future? Why?

B SCAN Read *The future of work* quickly. Which of your ideas from Exercise A are mentioned?

THE FUTURE OF WORK

Few people would argue that society hasn't [1]**benefited** enormously from technological advancements. However, the future of many jobs may be hanging in the [2]**balance** due to the increased use of robotics in the workplace. According to Osbourne and Frey from Oxford University, nearly 50% of jobs worldwide are at risk of being automated over the next 20 years. Taxi drivers could be replaced by driverless cars. In some warehouses, robots already move [3]**produce** around more efficiently than workers. Even the role of teachers could be dramatically affected as more and more of the learning process moves online. There's also a greater risk of change in certain countries where there are a high number of people employed in manufacturing. For example, the World Bank estimates that some countries risk up to 60% of jobs possibly being replaced by robots and automation, simply because technology is often able to [4]**produce** more than human workers, with better accuracy and attention to detail. Yet many economists argue that despite the risks of increased automation, there are still many opportunities and [5]**benefits** ahead.

Although to many this may feel like a new problem, in reality it is a [6]**challenge** that has existed for years. Since the invention of the printing press, machines have continued to replace humans in the workplace. In fact, people have always worried about technology taking their jobs. During the Industrial Revolution in England, the Luddites – a group of clothes and textile makers – protested against new technology in factories by destroying machinery. They weren't against the technology, but they didn't like the [7]**control** and power it gave to factory owners to make working conditions worse. In the late 1950s, there were also widespread protests across the USA in response to the [8]**influence** of automation on the shipping industry.

Although technological advances often [9]**challenge** society, overall levels of unemployment have never risen consistently. Periods of increased unemployment are usually temporary and associated with a recession. We don't run out of work – work simply changes and new jobs are created. People were once employed to open doors on trains and take people's tickets. Farmers, factory workers and lift operators have all lost their jobs due to technological changes. People have simply moved on and found new types of employment.

Automation will no doubt [10]**influence** society greatly as it starts to [11]**control** more and more aspects of our lives. However, arguably, it won't change the total number of jobs in the economy. Studies into the impact of automation on employment focus only on which existing jobs could be replaced. They do not address the subject of which new jobs might be created. While planes and boats may not have a crew on board, they will still need to be operated by someone remotely. As more and more of life moves online, we may find we need fewer traditional police officers and that experts in preventing online crime will become increasingly important. Jobs that we cannot even imagine at the moment will become vital.

While many of our jobs are no doubt under threat, it is a dramatic exaggeration to present the idea that huge numbers of people will find themselves unemployed because of automation. Humans will always be vital in the workforce, just not necessarily in ways we are used to. Technology may even free up humans to work less and allow them more free time to [12]**balance** the pressures of work, family and other interests.

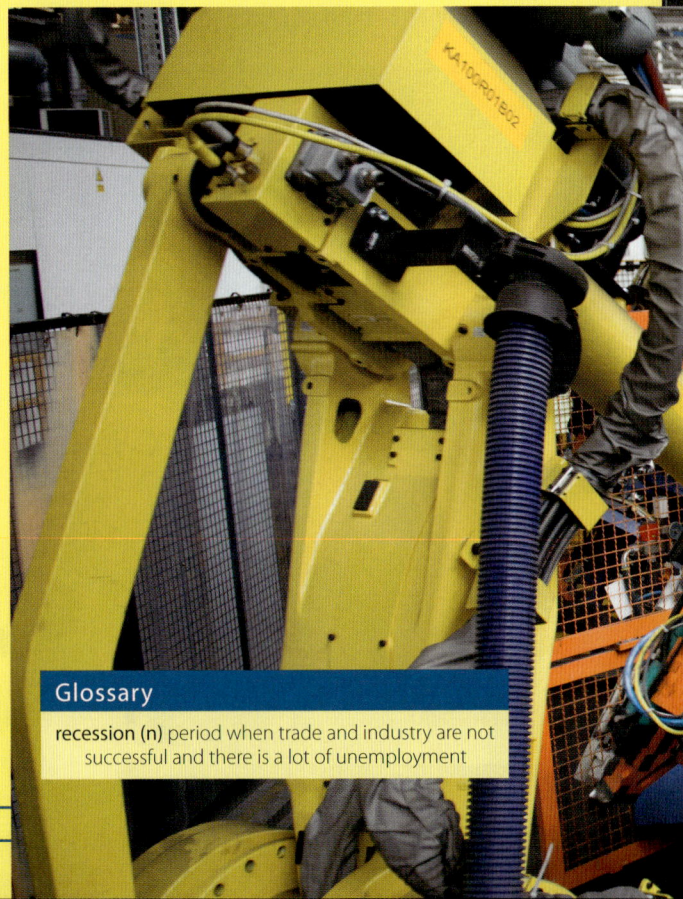

Glossary

recession (n) period when trade and industry are not successful and there is a lot of unemployment

C IDENTIFY EVIDENCE Read the article again. Underline the evidence used to support the arguments below. Use the information in the box to help you.

> **Identifying evidence**
>
> Good writers use evidence to support the argument or point they're trying to make. This can include references to specific studies, examples and statistics.

1 A large proportion of jobs are at risk from technological developments.

2 Some countries may suffer more than others due to automation.

3 Jobs have always been at risk from technological developments.

4 Many old jobs now no longer exist.

5 New jobs will be created that do not currently exist.

D SPEAK Work in pairs. Discuss the questions.

1 Do you think society needs to worry about automation affecting people's jobs? Why/Why not?

2 How might the increased use of robots and automation benefit society?

3 What skills do you think people need to develop to protect themselves from automation?

VOCABULARY
Nouns and verbs with the same spelling

A Scan the article again. Which of the words in bold (1–12) are nouns? Which are verbs?

B Complete the sentences with the correct form of the words in Exercise A.

1 One of the _____ of robotics could be more free time for individuals.

2 We need to _____ the convenience of automation with the need for employment.

3 We should constantly _____ companies that get away with paying lower taxes.

4 There's no doubt that technology _____ the way in which all industries work.

5 Some people think that automation gives companies more _____ over workers.

6 Robots make it quicker and easier for companies _____ their products.

PRONUNCIATION
Nouns and verbs with the same spelling

A Listen to the pairs of sentences. Are both forms of the words in bold pronounced the same way?
4.3

1 a The key **benefit** of increased automation is greater efficiency.

  b Technology should be used to **benefit** humans, not replace them.

2 a I think we'll all need to **upgrade** our skills.

  b This system is an **upgrade** on the previous one.

B Listen to the pairs of sentences. Underline the stressed syllable in each of the words in bold.
4.4

1 a An **increase** in automation will have a negative impact on jobs.

  b We need to **increase** the number of automated jobs in education.

2 a Robots are increasingly used to **produce** more and more products.

  b Lots of people are eating local **produce** to reduce their environmental impact.

3 a Many people would **reject** the idea of a machine being a doctor.

  b Products produced by machines usually lead to fewer **rejects** being made.

SPEAKING HUB

A PREPARE Would you be happy for a robot to do any of these jobs? Why/Why not? Make notes.

- a doctor
- a shop assistant
- a bus driver
- a teacher
- a waiter
- an accountant

B DISCUSS Work in groups. Discuss your ideas from Exercise A. Are there any other jobs that you think could or couldn't be automated?

C PRESENT Explain the main points of your discussion to the class. Which jobs do you think could be automated? Which couldn't? Why?

○ – Talk about future plans and goals
○ – Make predictions about the future of work

G – future perfect simple, future continuous and future perfect continuous

S – identifying agreement and disagreement   **V** – intensifiers   **P** – intonation with intensifiers

READING

A SPEAK Work in groups. Discuss which of the following will become common within the next decade.

- driverless cars
- virtual reality in the classroom
- space tourism
- 3D printing in the home

B PREDICT Work in pairs. Look at the subheadings in *When science fiction becomes science fact*. What predictions do you think each section will make about the future?

C READ FOR GIST Read the article quickly. Which of your ideas from Exercise B are mentioned?

D IDENTIFY OPINION Read the article again. Write Y (Yes) if the statement agrees with the writer's opinion. Write N (No) if it contradicts the writer's opinion. Write NG (Not Given) if it is impossible to say what the writer thinks.

1 The author thinks pollution is the main threat to cities. ___
2 AI and robotics will dominate both our home and work lives. ___
3 Humans and robots will work side by side. ___
4 Social media will affect people's real-life status. ___
5 People will have little contact with each other. ___
6 We need laws to restrict the influence of social media. ___

WHEN
SCIENCE FICTION
BECOMES
SCIENCE FACT

In 1989, the film *Back to the Future 2* predicted that 26 years into the future, people would make video calls, use wearable technology and tablet computers, and play video games hands-free. Whilst these predictions probably seemed pretty unrealistic at the time, all have come true in some form or another. Even the famous hoverboard could soon become a reality, as car giant Lexus have recently developed a working prototype. So, are predictions made in film and TV always this accurate? Here we take a look at some of the key predictions made in science fiction over the past 30 years and assess which, if any, are likely to come true.

ENVIRONMENT

Many films set in the future show changes to our environment. *Blade Runner* is set in the year 2049 and shows a dark future in which pollution levels in the city are shockingly high, and the sun is rarely seen. The natural environment has been almost completely destroyed and industrial cities dominate the landscape. While this film focuses on the pollution and poor air quality in major cities, in reality the biggest environmental threat to cities is arguably rising sea levels. Recent estimates suggest that if we are unable to dramatically reduce the amount of carbon dioxide released into the atmosphere over the next few decades, [1] sea levels will have risen so much by 2050 that hundreds of millions of people will lose their homes. At present, the city most affected would be Shanghai. Projections show that the majority of the city will disappear under water if global temperatures increase by just three degrees.

TECHNOLOGY

Perhaps the most common types of prediction made in films centre around technology. According to Alex Proyas's film *I, Robot*, by 2035 robots will have evolved to such a point that they will be able to carry out most human tasks.

[2] By 2035, we will have been living with computers for around 100 years, and while many predictions estimate that robots will be doing nearly 50% of jobs worldwide within the next 20 years, a world like Proyas's is still a long way from reality. [3] It is much more likely robots will be working alongside humans, rather than replacing them.

E SPEAK Work in groups. Discuss the questions.

1 Which of the predictions in the article do you think will come true? Why?

2 What else do you think might happen in each of the categories over the next twenty years?

GRAMMAR
Future perfect simple, future continuous and future perfect continuous

A Scan the article again. Match the highlighted sentences (1–3) to the things they describe (a–c).

a an action or situation that will be finished before a specific time in the future ___

b an action or situation that will continue up to a specific time in the future ___

c an action or situation that will be in progress at a specific time in the future ___

COMMUNICATION

Movies are also full of predictions about the future of communication. The communicators in *Star Trek* are incredibly similar to modern mobile phones, and the 1927 classic *Metropolis* showed video calls long before the creation of Skype. Our increased reliance on smartphones is taken a step further in the film *Her*, where the main character has a relationship with a computer operating system that has a female voice.

If it's still popular in 2025, we will have been using Facebook for just over twenty years. The Netflix series *Black Mirror* shows a future where the 'like' feature of Facebook impacts on people's actual lives. The more likes someone gets, the higher their social status is in real life. As a result they can get better cars, houses and jobs. Although this is unlikely to happen, it does draw our attention to the worrying impact of social media on society.

B WORK IT OUT Scan the text again and complete the box with one more example of each tense.

> **Future perfect simple, future continuous and future perfect continuous**
>
> We use the **future perfect simple** to talk about something that will finish before a specific point of time in the future.
> 1 _____
>
> We use the **future continuous** to talk about an action or situation that will be in progress at a specific time in the future.
> 2 _____
>
> We use the **future perfect continuous** to talk about an action or situation that will continue up to a specific time in the future.
> 3 _____

C Go to the Grammar Hub on page XII.

D PRACTISE Complete the predictions with the future perfect simple, future continuous or future perfect continuous form of the verbs in brackets.

1 I _____ (change) jobs by the end of the year.

2 I _____ (live) in the same place in thirty years' time.

3 I _____ (visit) five new countries by the end of the decade.

4 By the end of the month, I _____ (buy) a new phone.

5 By the end of the decade, I _____ (work) for the same company for over twenty years.

6 In five years' time, I _____ (still / study) English.

E SPEAK Work in pairs. Which predictions in Exercise D do you think will become true for you? Why?

SPEAKING

A PREPARE Read the following predictions from different science fiction films. Which do you think will become true? Make notes.

Police will be able to predict the future, preventing serious crimes before they happen. *Minority Report* (2002)

You will be able to pay to have your memory of a relationship that went wrong permanently erased. *Eternal Sunshine of a Spotless Mind* (2004)

Humans will learn how to communicate with aliens. *Arrival* (2016)

The Earth will be so damaged that humans will look for a new planet to call home. *Interstellar* (2014)

The rich will control cities from high-rise towers, whilst the poor will work machines underground. *Metropolis* (1927).

B SPEAK Work in pairs. Compare your ideas from Exercise A. Explain your reasoning.

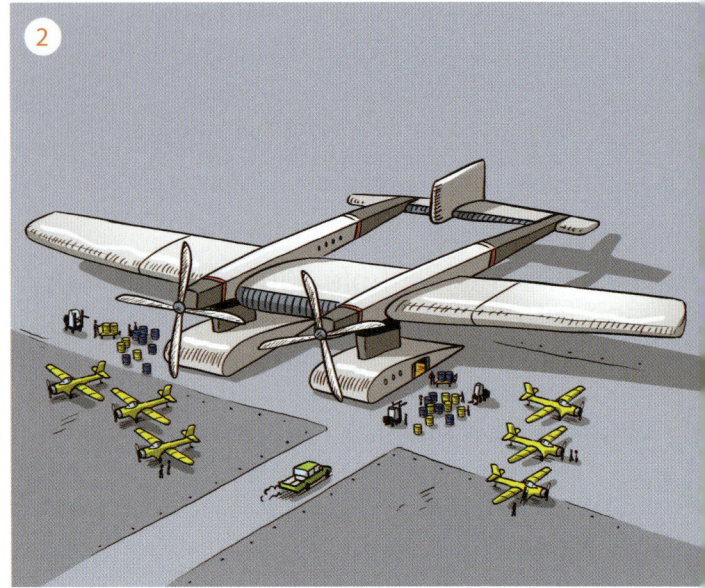

LISTENING

A SPEAK Work in pairs. Look at the pictures (1–3) and discuss the questions.

1 Which of the predictions about future transport came true?

2 Which didn't come true and why do you think they failed?

3 How do you think transport will change over the next ten years?

B LISTEN FOR GIST Listen to a public debate about the future of transport. Put the modes of transport in the order they are discussed.

4.5

___ hypersonic jets   ___ driverless cars

___ hyperloop trains   ___ flying bikes

C IDENTIFY AGREEMENT AND DISAGREEMENT Listen again. Who makes the following points – Mark or Sarah? To what extent to they agree with each other? Use the information in the box to help you.

4.5

> ### Identifying agreement and disagreement
>
> When arguing about a topic, speakers use expressions such as *I completely agree*, *I can't see …*, *Yes, but …*, etc to signal agreement or disagreement. These are often followed by reasons and examples to counter or support the original point.
>
> Speakers also highlight agreement or disagreement by responding with a single adverb (e.g. *Seriously?*, *Definitely!*, etc).

1 Driverless cars will soon become a common sight on our roads.

2 Driverless cars have better reactions than human drivers.

3 Hyperloops are safer than existing train systems.

4 Hyperloop train systems are unlikely to get the funding they need.

5 We're unlikely to develop flying cars within the next two decades.

6 There may be a market for space tourism in the future.

D SPEAK Work in pairs. Read the driverless car scenario Sarah describes in the discussion. What do you think the car should do? Explain your reasoning.

How can a car make a decision about what to do in a dangerous situation? Should it protect the driver at all costs? What if doing so might mean injuring somebody else? What does it do then? I just think it would be incredibly dangerous to have driverless cars on the road.

VOCABULARY
Intensifiers

A Read the extracts from the discussion. Complete the definitions below with the words in bold.

1 The way we get around is going to be **entirely** transformed.

2 I **firmly** believe there is no chance driverless cars will become popular.

3 It's **undoubtedly** true that driverless cars will have more consistent and quicker reactions than most drivers.

4 But it would **greatly** improve our lives!

5 Hyperloop train systems are **widely** expected to happen.

6 … **especially** things that save significant time, like the Hyperloop train…

7 … it will become **significantly** cheaper over time.

8 You seem **incredibly** focused on speed!

a _____ completely, or in every way

b _____ in a way that is relevant or that has an important effect on something

c _____ used for saying that something is certainly true or is accepted by everyone

d _____ very much

e _____ extremely

f _____ by a lot of people, or in a lot of places

g _____ strongly

h _____ used when mentioning conditions that make something more relevant, important or true

B Choose the correct intensifiers to complete the sentences.

1 Many of these inventions seem *undoubtedly / incredibly* unlikely to happen.

2 It's *entirely / greatly* possible that all cars will be driverless in the future.

3 There are *significantly / firmly* more passengers using the system than it was designed for originally.

4 Travel times would be *greatly / entirely* improved.

5 You are *undoubtedly / especially* right.

6 I *firmly / widely* believe that safety is more important than convenience.

7 That is *especially / widely* true when it comes to a company making a profit.

8 It is *significantly / widely* believed that commercial flights will eventually be powered by solar energy.

C Go to the **Vocabulary Hub** on **page XIX**.

D **SPEAK** Work in pairs. Use intensifiers to give your opinions on the topics below.

- the likelihood of space tourism
- police travelling by hover bikes
- the widespread use of hyperloop trains

Space tourism in our lifetime seems incredibly unlikely.

PRONUNCIATION
Intonation with intensifiers

A Listen to the extract from the debate. What intonation does the speaker use on the intensifiers: rising (↗), falling (↘) or rise-fall (↗↘)? What effect does this have?
4.6

They're ==undoubtedly== cheaper than building a normal high-speed train and travel times will be ==greatly== reduced.

B Listen and repeat the sentences.
4.7

1 The city is incredibly congested!

2 The idea is entirely unrealistic. It will never happen.

3 Considering the environmental impact has become increasingly important.

4 Travel times will be greatly reduced.

SPEAKING HUB

A **PLAN** Read the information cards and make notes about the advantages and disadvantages of each form of transport.

🚆 CITY TRAIN

Completion:	2030
Design:	Spacious and modern. Inbuilt wi-fi. First-class meeting tables
Cost:	£5 billion
Ticket cost:	£10 day ticket
Speed:	Much faster than road vehicles. Delays less likely

🚌 ECO BUS

Completion:	2022
Design:	Eco-friendly using renewable energy
Cost:	£300 million
Ticket cost:	£3 day ticket
Speed:	Faster than cars as uses a designated bus lane. Delays possible

🚋 TRAM SYSTEM

Completion:	2025
Design:	A simple underground train. Many roads will need to be redesigned to fit trams
Cost:	£2 billion
Ticket cost:	£5 day ticket
Speed:	Relatively slow-moving. Delays possible

B **PREPARE** Work in three groups. You are going to propose a new transport system for your city. Group A – City Train, Group B – Eco Bus, Group C – Tram System. Prepare you arguments.

C **DISCUSS** Debate the best method as a class. Remember to question the weaknesses in the other methods.

○– **Evaluate future predictions**
○– **Debate a range of transport proposals**

▶ Flippy the robot

COMPREHENSION

A Work in pairs. You are going to watch a news report about a burger-flipping robot. What do you think the advantages and disadvantages of this kind of technology are?

B ▶ Watch the report. Which of your ideas from Exercise A are mentioned?

C ▶ Watch again. Complete the sentences with no more than three words from the report.

1 A combination of image recognition and _____ _____ tells Flippy which burgers need turning over.

2 The introduction of Flippy may lead to _____ _____ in the future.

3 CaliBurger will spend an estimated _____ _____ a year on maintenance.

4 Human employees often find the working conditions difficult and many leave after _____ _____.

5 Flippy isn't fully autonomous yet and regularly _____ _____ that a human employee wouldn't.

6 David Zito, the CEO of Miso Robotics, is confident that Flippy _____ with time.

7 The presenter believes it won't be long before Flippy can both _____ and serve customers.

8 Roboticists predict that new _____ _____ will emerge to replace those lost.

D Work in groups. Do you agree with the following predictions made in the report? Why/Why not?

1 It won't be long before the majority of unskilled jobs are automated.

2 In the future, it will be odd to go to a restaurant that isn't almost fully automated.

AUTHENTIC ENGLISH

A Read the extract from the report. Why do you think the speaker says *right*?

It's not a very fun job, **right**? Er, it's hot, it's greasy, it's dirty, erm, it hurts your wrist, **right**?

B Read the information in the box and check your answers to Exercise A.

---

right
In informal spoken English, speakers often use *right* in place of a question tag to check information or to ask if someone agrees with them.

*You've got tomorrow off, **right?***
(= You've got tomorrow off, haven't you?)

*You know where you're going, **right?***
(= You know where you're going, don't you?)

C Read the extract in Exercise A again. Which regular question tags could be used instead of *right*?

D Work in pairs. Take turns using prompts (1–6) to make sentences with *right*.

1 You want to check that the film starts at 9 pm.

2 You think your friend has met Yuki before.

3 You're not sure if a friend can speak Japanese.

4 You think a colleague is going to Seville next week.

5 You think a friend finishes early on Fridays.

6 You want to check your friend knows how to get to the station.

So, the film starts at 9 pm, right?

▶ The perfect coffee

SAM   MALCOLM   AMANDA   HARRY   EMILY

A Work in pairs. What's your favourite café? Why do you like it so much?

B ▶ Watch the video. Choose the best summary (1–3) of what Sam thinks customers want from an independent café.

1 They want to be served quickly and efficiently.

2 They want to make use of the latest technology.

3 They want to feel like a valued part of a community.

SPEAKING SKILL

A ▶ Watch the video again. Complete the box with examples from the conversation.

Asking for clarification

In conversation, we often need to check that we have understood something correctly. A common way to do this is to use a signalling phrase followed by an explanation of what we think the speaker meant.

Sam: I want the people who come to our café to feel that it is their space. So I often allow local clubs to hold meetings here or we host events like book signings or talks.

*Amanda: **So you mean that** the café can be a hub for the local community?*

We use a number of other phrases for asking for clarification, some of which are more formal than others:

More formal

1 _____

2 _____

Less formal

3 _____

4 _____

B Work in pairs. Tell your partner about your job or a job you would like to have. Listen to your partner and ask for clarification of what they tell you. Then swap roles.

Talk about:

- what skills and knowledge you need
- who you work with
- what you like/dislike about the job
- what your responsibilities are
- what equipment you use

SPEAKING HUB

A PREPARE Work in pairs. You are going to conduct an interview about increased automation in the restaurant industry.

Student A – You are a journalist. Choose which questions to ask from the list below and add some of your own.

Student B – You are the interviewee. Make notes about your responses to the questions below.

- How might the industry benefit from increased automation?
- Which jobs do you think are most at risk from this trend?
- How do you think the public would react?

B SPEAK Conduct the interview. Ask each other for clarification if you need to.

Correct me if I'm wrong, but you seem to be saying that you'd be happy for robots to help prepare, but not serve your food. Is that right?

C DISCUSS As a class, discuss whether increased automation in the workplace is mainly positive or negative.

◯ **Give your opinion on automation in the workplace**

➤ Turn to page XXVII to learn how to write a for and against blog post.

VOCABULARY

A Choose the correct prepositions to complete the sentences.

1 I want to take a course *in / on / for* accounting next year.

2 There's a risk *with / of / for* the company going out of business before the end of the year.

3 Do you have any knowledge *of / in / on* spreadsheets?

4 Congratulations *about / for / on* the birth of your new baby daughter!

5 There are lots of historic places of interest *at / in / on* the north of the country.

6 Is there any possibility *for / of / about* getting a refund?

B Complete the sentences with words from the box.

> balance   benefit   challenge
> control   influence   produce

1 We are being expected _____ far more than is humanly possible!

2 I'm so exhausted all the time. I think I just need a better work–life _____.

3 Always _____ yourself to try something new is extremely important.

4 The trend towards digital _____ the new direction of the company.

5 If this deal goes through, XKOM _____ 65% of the market.

6 One of the _____ of exercise is that it lowers your stress levels.

C Choose the correct options (a, b or c) to complete the sentences.

1 He often exaggerates so I'm not ___ sure I believe him.
   a entirely   **b** firmly   **c** widely

2 They've ___ improved the new model.
   a entirely   **b** incredibly   **c** significantly

3 ___, everyone survived the plane crash.
   a Undoubtedly **b** Incredibly   **c** Widely

4 The price of tickets may vary ___ between distributors.
   a firmly   **b** greatly   **c** especially

5 I ___ believe that closing the company was the right decision to make.
   a firmly   **b** widely   **c** significantly

6 New England is often pretty cold, ___ in winter.
   a greatly   **b** incredibly   **c** especially

7 The population will ___ continue to rise as more people move there for work.
   a incredibly   **b** undoubtedly **c** firmly

8 It is ___ believed that AI will place many jobs at risk.
   a widely   **b** especially   **c** entirely

GRAMMAR

A Complete the article with *will*, *going to* or the present continuous form of the verbs in brackets. Sometimes more than one answer is possible.

Four **changes** to make to your **life**

At the start of every year, we all make promises to change certain aspects of our life. 'I ¹_____ (*do*) more exercise' and 'I ²_____ (*eat*) more healthily' we say. But so often we fail to keep our promises. So what simple changes can we make that will make a big difference and be easy to achieve?

❶ Get up and go to sleep at the same time. You ³_____ (*feel*) a lot more refreshed.

❷ Be punctual. It reduces stress. If you start arriving early for things, you ⁴_____ (*find*) that life starts to feel less frantic.

❸ Routine is good, but you should also be spontaneous occasionally. When a friend says, 'I ⁵_____ (*go*) the seaside this weekend, do you want to come?' Say, 'Great! I ⁶_____ (*come*).'

❹ Try to be optimistic. For example, if your company is struggling, don't think 'I ⁷_____ (*lose*) my job.' Be positive and think about the new good job you might get.

Make these simple changes in your life and I am sure you ⁸_____ (*be*) happier in the long run.

B Choose the correct options to complete the sentences.

1 Can we meet later? I *'ll be watching / 'll have watched* the cup final then.

2 At the end of this month, I *'ll be working / 'll have been working* at this company for 20 years!

3 Just think – this time next week, we *'ll be lying / 'll have been lying* on a beach in Hawaii.

4 I can't believe she's changing jobs again. She *'ll have had / 'll be having* three different jobs this year!

5 I *won't be finishing / won't have finished* this work by the deadline. I just don't have enough time.

6 *Will you be going / Will you have gone* to Sarah's party on Saturday?

7 In three years' time, I *'ll have completed / 'll be completing* university and I'll be starting to look for work.

8 This is ridiculous! In ten minutes time I *'ll have been waiting / 'll be waiting* for nearly two hours!

CHANGE

I cannot say whether things will get better
if we change; what I can say is that they
must change if they are to get better.

Georg C. Lichtenberg

A traditional roof against a modern skyscraper in Seoul, South Korea.

OBJECTIVES

- summarise a sequence of past events
- evaluate a range of proposals
- talk about changes in your town or city
- evaluate candidates and put together a team
- discuss ways to help the environment
- write a problem solution article

Work with a partner. Discuss the questions.

1 Read the quote. What do you think
Lichtenberg means? Do you agree
with him? Why/Why not?

2 What are the biggest changes in the world
that have happened in your lifetime?

3 What is the most positive change you have
ever made?

READING

A SPEAK Work in pairs. Look at the food chain diagram and discuss the questions.

1 What does the diagram show?

2 In this diagram, the wolf is the top predator. What do you think that means?

3 What would happen if you removed the wolf from this food chain? Why?

B SCAN Read *How wolves change rivers* quickly and check your answers to Exercise A.

The Yellowstone Food Chain

Vegetation → Elk → Grey Wolf

HOW WOLVES CHANGE RIVERS

Wolves are top predators and their beneficial effects on entire ecosystems <u>are gradually being understood</u>.

Wolves are crucial for maintaining a healthy ecosystem – a fact that many people overlooked when they were being hunted and killed in vast numbers across the United States at the start of the 20th century.

Meanwhile, the populations of other animals exploded. The entire ecosystem of the American countryside changed as a result of rapidly expanding populations of elk.

After years of political discussion, conservation biologists finally got their way and the grey wolf, *Canis lupus*, was reintroduced to several areas in the northern Rocky Mountains of the United States. One of those areas was Yellowstone National Park.

Although researchers only reintroduced a total of 41 wolves to the park, their beneficial influences soon became clear, and continue to be seen to this day. As wolves are top predators that mainly hunt sick or ageing elk, their reintroduction had two main effects. Firstly, it slowed the expansion of the elk population, which had exploded without natural predators. Secondly, it actually improved the overall health of the elk population as only the strongest and fittest survived.

The presence of wolves even changed elk behaviours. For example, they stopped eating in valleys where they could easily be attacked by wolves. Because of this, native plants were able to regrow, increasing biodiversity by providing food and shelter to a growing variety of plants and animals.

Amazingly, the presence of wolves also changed many rivers in the park. After the reintroduction of the wolves, researchers noticed that riverbanks became stronger, the rivers became deeper and small pools formed. Why? Again, the plants that had been eaten by the elk had time to recover, strengthening the riverbanks and in turn, changing the geography of the park itself.

Basically, humans conducted a huge real-life experiment by removing and then reintroducing a top predator from a large area of land. Initially, the changes caused by the lack of wolves were too small to be noticed. But the results of their reintroduction clearly indicate that wolves are essential to restoring and maintaining the ecosystem of the entire region.

This type of relationship is known as a 'trophic cascade'. In Yellowstone National Park, researchers observed the effect when the removal of the top predator started a chain of effects that affected the entire web of life. Similar effects have been identified throughout the natural world, from the Amazon rainforest to the eastern Pacific Ocean.

As more species are reintroduced around the world, no doubt more will be learned about the impact each has not just on ecosystems, but also on the surrounding landscapes.

Glossary

biodiversity (n) the variety of different types of plant and animal life in a particular region

ecosystem (n) all the living things in an area and how they affect each other and the environment

predator (n) an animal that kills and eats other animals

C IDENTIFY CAUSE AND EFFECT Read the article again. Are the sentences true (T) or false (F)? Correct the false sentences. Use the information in the box to help you.

Identifying cause and effect

Texts often indicate a cause and effect relationship between different events. These relationships are usually signalled by fixed phrases such as *cause, bring about, lead to, as a result of, the main consequence was*, etc.

1 Wolves started to die out because there were not enough elk to eat. T / F
2 Growing elk numbers affected all the other plants and animals. T / F
3 Reintroducing wolves meant elk populations grew. T / F
4 Reintroducing wolves made elk populations healthier. T / F
5 A wider range of plants started to grow again as wolf numbers grew. T / F
6 The regrowth of plants meant that rivers became deeper. T / F

D SPEAK Work in groups. What animals are in danger of extinction in your country? What is being done about it?

GRAMMAR
The passive

A Scan the article again and underline ten examples of the passive. The first has been underlined for you.

B SPEAK Work in pairs. Discuss the questions.
1 What tenses are the examples in Exercise A?
2 Which include a modal verb?
3 Which are in the infinitive form?

C WORK IT OUT Choose the correct options to complete the rules.

The passive

We form the passive with *be* + [1]*past simple / past participle*.

The passive can be formed with [2]*all / some* tenses – only the form of *be* changes.

We use the passive when:
- we [3]*know / don't know* who or what caused an action
- it's [4]*important / not important* who or what caused an action
- we want to focus on the person or thing that [5]*did the action / received the action*.

D PRACTISE Complete the sentences with the correct passive form of the verbs in brackets.

1 As the population continues to grow, more and more land _____ (use) for farming.
2 Very few fossil fuels _____ (burn) before the Industrial Revolution.
3 Thousands of trees _____ (cut down) every year before the government changed the law.
4 The future of humans _____ (could / threaten) by further increases in temperature.
5 Many species _____ (affect) by climate change over the decade.
6 Plastic bags _____ (ban) recently in many countries.
7 Global temperatures _____ (rise) for over a century.
8 Some people feel that the use of packaging needs _____ (control).

E Go to the Grammar Hub on page XIV.

SPEAKING

A PREPARE Go to the Communication Hub on page XXII.

B DISCUSS Work in pairs. What are the main predators in your country? What other animals would be affected if they became extinct?

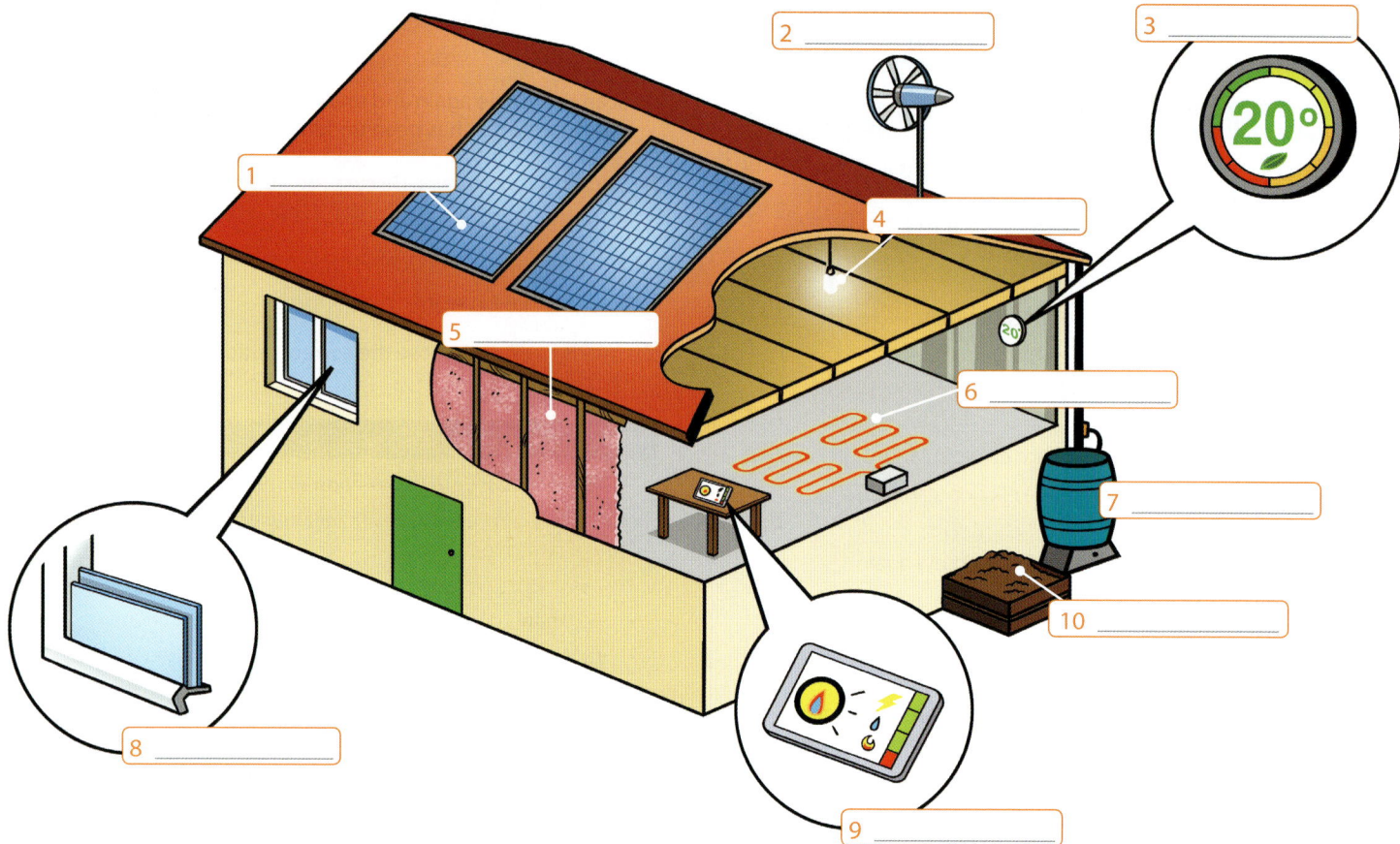

VOCABULARY
Green vocabulary

A Label the picture with words in the box.

compost heap   double glazing   energy-efficient lightbulb
insulation   smart meter   solar panels   thermostat
underfloor heating   water butt   wind turbine

B Complete the sentences with words from Exercise A.

1 Turning down your _____ by just one degree can save money and energy.

2 Using _____ to produce energy from the sun can save you money.

3 _____ can be used to extract heat stored in the ground through the floor of the house.

4 _____ last much longer and use less energy than traditional ones.

5 Use a _____ to capture rain which can then be used in the garden and the toilet system.

6 Families often throw away a lot of food that could instead have been put in a _____.

7 Using a _____ can produce clean energy on windy days.

8 Installing a _____ helps keep track of energy use and may even save money.

9 Since warm air rises, it is important that you have _____ to keep the heat in.

10 _____ is much better at keeping heat in than traditional windows are.

C SPEAK Work in pairs. Which of these do you have in your home? Which would you install if you had the money?

LISTENING

A LISTEN FOR KEY WORDS Listen to a radio interview about an eco-friendly home. Which of the features in the vocabulary section are not mentioned?
5.1

B LISTEN FOR DETAIL Listen again. Complete the sentences with no more than four words from the interview.
5.1

1 Harry is making changes because he was surprised by his _____.

2 He made simple changes himself, such as putting _____ in each room and fitting _____.

3 The solar panels make _____ _____ of the energy he needs.

4 The beehive means the roof is a source of _____ as well as energy.

5 The water butt now means the _____ _____ uses rainwater.

6 The underfloor heating helps lower Harry's _____.

7 The smart fridge means they _____ _____.

8 The new shower _____ to save water and energy.

GRAMMAR
Causative *have* and *get*

🔊 **A** Listen and complete the extracts from the interview.
5.2

1 Ah, I can see you're _____ solar panels _____.

2 We're _____ underfloor heating _____.

3 We need _____ the walls better _____.

B **PRACTISE** Complete the sentences using the prompts in brackets. Use the information in the box to help you.

> ### Causative *have* and *get*
>
> We use the causative *have* and *get* (*have / get* + object + past participle) to say that someone does something for us – often for tasks we can't or don't know how to do ourselves. Compare these sentences:
>
> *Camille is installing solar panels on her roof.* (= she is doing it herself.)
>
> *Camille is having solar panels installed on her roof.* (= someone is installing them for her.)

1 I _____ (*have / the car / repair*) at the garage last weekend.

2 We're _____ (*get / the house / paint*) at the moment.

3 We're also _____ (*have / a smart energy meter / fit*) to check how much energy we're using.

4 We _____ (*have / a roof garden / create*) last year to help keep heat in.

5 I'd like _____ (*get / new flooring / install*) in the living room.

C Go to the **Grammar Hub** on **page XIV**.

PRONUNCIATION
Glottal stops

🔊 **A** Listen to the extract from the interview. Is the /t/ in the highlighted words pronounced or not pronounced?
5.3

We're also getting a <mark>smart</mark> meter installed. Hopefully, <mark>it'll</mark> help us keep an eye on how much – or how little – energy we're using!

🔊 **B** Listen and repeat the sentences.
5.4

1 It's a great way to save money on your bills.

2 We'd like to start growing our own food.

3 We should save about £100 a year.

4 We need to get quotes for the underfloor heating.

⭘ SPEAKING HUB

A **PLAN** A local school has £30,000 to spend to make the school more environmentally friendly. Make notes about the advantages and disadvantages of each idea.

> 🌱 **ORGANIC GARDEN**
> Cost £500. The food grown could be served in the school canteen and save the school £300 a year. It would mean less playground space for the children.

> 📘 **DOUBLE GLAZING**
> Cost £25,000. This would save the school £2000 a year in heating bills. The installation would take a long time and some classrooms couldn't be used for a while.

> 🌬 **WIND TURBINES**
> Cost £10,000. There is the potential to save £1000 per year but the school is not in a very windy location.

> ☀ **SOLAR PANELS**
> Cost £16,000. There is the potential to save £1400 per year and the school is in a sunny location.

> 🚽 **WATER SAVING TOILETS**
> Cost £3000. This solution won't save the school any money, but it will reduce waste water a lot.

> 💡 **ENERGY SAVING BULBS**
> Cost £300. Saving the school £60 per year. This solution is quick and easy to implement.

B **DISCUSS** Work in groups. Discuss how to spend the £30,000. Explain your reasoning.

C **PRESENT** Explain which options you chose in Exercise B and why.

⭘– **Summarise a sequence of past events**
⭘– **Evaluate a range of proposals**

5.2 Changing places

● Talk about changes in your town or city
● Evaluate candidates and put together a team

V — describing areas of a city; prefixes
P — words that lose a syllable
S — listening for rhetorical questions
G — *-ing* and infinitive forms

READING

A PREDICT Work in pairs. Look at the pictures of Dubai. What do you think causes a city to grow so quickly? What do you think the effects of such quick growth are?

B SCAN Scan *Rise of the megacities* and check your predictions from Exercise A.

C READ FOR ORGANISATION Read the article again. Complete the gaps (1–6) with the sentences (a–f).

a Gyeonggi, on the southern outskirts of the city, has gained more than five million residents in the last 30 years.

b Today, it is a city of over a million but 60 years ago, its population was under 20,000.

c However, in recent years, rapid urbanisation has been happening at a rate never seen before.

d Unfortunately, for many people, especially in poorer countries, this has not always been the case.

e At the heart of this rapid expansion in urban populations are the same factors that have been there for centuries.

f So, where and why is this happening at such an astounding rate?

D SPEAK Work in pairs. What are the main advantages and disadvantages of living in a major city?

Rise of the
MEGACITIES

Large cities are not a new phenomenon. Attracted by work, better facilities and living standards, there have been cities with a population of over a million people for around 2000 years. ¹___ This is particularly evident in the Middle East and across Asia, where many cities have swelled to populations in excess of ten million. Places that even just a few decades ago were nothing more than small farming towns or fishing villages now have millions of people living in them. ²___

Seoul, in South Korea, is a prosperous **urban** area today, but in the 1950s it was a much poorer and smaller place. Once Seoul began to expand, much of the population growth was in the central **commercial** area. This has changed in the last 20 or 30 years, as much of the growth has been in the **suburbs**, where huge **residential** areas have been built on the edge of the city. ³___ Overpopulation has meant redeveloping traditional **industrial** areas of the city, where vast **housing** projects have expanded the population greatly. Although the growth of Seoul has been extraordinary, it has been a large city for decades. Abu Dhabi, on the other hand, was once not much more than a small village, and has grown immensely in recent times. ⁴___ It is not the only city to grow at this rapid rate, so what has led to this rapid expansion?

Population growth in general has come about due to falling death rates and improved life expectancy, but city populations are growing for numerous reasons. ⁵___ High levels of unemployment and a lack of resources have always pushed people away from **rural** areas. There is a perception that life will be better in a city, as the future residents are attracted to the prospect of well-paid jobs, greater opportunities to find work, better health care and education. ⁶___ All too many cities have illegal **slums** with poor living conditions, little or no electricity and limited access to clean drinking water. Yet this does not seem to deter new residents as both the central area and suburban populations continue to expand.

The trend of urbanisation is unlikely to slow down any time soon, with millions of people expected to move to urban areas in the future, no doubt creating more megacities in the process. From Bogota to Chengdu, the march of the megacities shows no signs of stopping across the world.

VOCABULARY
Describing areas of a city

A Scan the article again. Complete the definitions with the words in bold.

1 _____ (n) an area where people live that is outside the city centre

2 _____ (adj) relating to industry

3 _____ (adj) relating to towns and cities, or happening there

4 _____ (n) a poor area of a town where the houses are in very bad condition

5 _____ (adj) relating to where people live rather than work

6 _____ (n) buildings for people to live in

7 _____ (adj) relating to business

8 _____ (adj) relating to or in the countryside

B Choose the correct options (a, b or c) to complete the sentences.

1 Over half of the world's population live in ___ areas and this is expected to grow.
   a urban   b commercial   c slums

2 Depopulation in ___ areas has led to even less work and fewer facilities.
   a commercial   b suburb   c rural

3 The ___ area is home to some of the largest banks and financial companies in the world.
   a industrial   b commercial   c residential

4 When people have families, they often move to the ___ to have more space.
   a suburbs   b housing   c residential

5 ___ areas with good transport connections are often more expensive to live in.
   a Slum   b Industrial   c Residential

6 A lack of affordable ___ can lead to people living in poor conditions.
   a suburbs   b housing   c slums

7 When traditionally ___ areas are in decline, many of the old factories are often converted to flats.
   a industrial   b commercial   c rural

8 The biggest ___ in the world has over half a million people living in poor quality housing.
   a suburb   b slum   c urban

C **SPEAK** Work in pairs. Use the words in Exercise A to describe your city or a city you know well.

PRONUNCIATION
Words that lose a syllable

A How many syllables are there in the underlined words? Write the number next to each sentence. Then listen and check. *5.5*

1 There are <u>reasonable</u> transport connections in the area. ___

2 There has been a <u>considerable</u> rise in the cost of living. ___

3 <u>Traditionally</u>, industrial areas have been converted into housing. ___

B Cross out the syllables that are not pronounced in the sentences below. Then listen and check. *5.6*

1 It's preferable to live in a central area as the shopping is better.

2 Much has changed, especially in terms of the transport system.

3 My personal preference is to live near the transport network.

VOCABULARY
Prefixes

> **Prefixes**
>
> Prefixes are added to the start of a word to change the meaning. For example, *mega-* is added to the start of a word to mean *very big or important* (e.g. *megacity*).

A Complete the words in bold with a prefix from the box.

> extra- il- over- re- sub- un-

1 The cost of housing has led to some _____**legal** housing areas being built.

2 There have been some _____**ordinary** new buildings constructed in the centre of the city.

3 _____**population** has become a problem in my city.

4 They have _____**developed** the old industrial area of the city.

5 The _____**urban** areas around the city have expanded rapidly.

6 Many were _____**happy** about the construction of a large supermarket on the site.

B Go to the **Vocabulary Hub** on **page XIX**.

SPEAKING

A **PREPARE** Make notes about important changes in your town or city over the past ten years. Think about:

- transport
- the cost of living
- shopping
- housing

B **SPEAK** Work in pairs. Tell your partner about how your town or city has changed.

C **DISCUSS** Work in pairs. Discuss the questions.

1 Do you think the changes in your city have been mostly positive or negative? Why?

2 What changes would you like to see in the future?

LISTENING

A SPEAK Work in pairs. Read the FAQs page and discuss the questions.

1 What is Mars One?

2 Would you qualify to be a Mars One astronaut?

3 Would you like to apply? Why/Why not?

4 What do you think you would find most difficult about being a Mars One astronaut?

B LISTEN FOR MAIN IDEA Listen to three radio interviews with Mars One candidates. Answer the questions with A (Agatha), T (Tim) or B (Bernie).

5.7

Who …

1 is confident about their physical ability? ___

2 would miss the city atmosphere? ___

3 thinks their attitude and work experience are important? ___

4 is going to have little contact with others to prepare for the mission? ___

5 would miss having a normal life? ___

6 is worried about losing part of their morning routine? ___

C LISTEN FOR RHETORICAL QUESTIONS Listen again. Tick (✓) the questions that are used rhetorically. Use the information in the box to help you.

5.7

Listening for rhetorical questions

A rhetorical question is a question asked for effect, not because the speaker expects an answer. They are often used to emphasise when the speaker thinks something is obvious, or to express surprise, doubt or agreement.

- [ ] Isn't that scary?
- [ ] Surely, being a scientist is the most important thing you bring to the team?
- [ ] Can you prepare yourself?
- [ ] Can anyone live without coffee?
- [ ] Shall we take a short break?
- [ ] Who doesn't enjoy a challenge?
- [ ] Why would I be scared?

D INFER MEANING Work in groups. Tim says that 'everyone wants to leave their mark behind'. What do you think he means by this? How do you want to make your mark?

E SPEAK Work in small groups. Discuss which candidate you would choose for the mission and why.

MISSION TO MARS

FAQS

What is the Mars One project?

The Mars One project was founded in 2011 with the aim of starting a human settlement on Mars.

How will candidates be selected?

Candidates will be selected through online applications, interviews, group challenges and simulations.

How old must candidates be?

The selection process is open to anyone over the age of 18.

What physical requirements are there?

Candidates must be healthy and have a good level of fitness. They must be between 157 and 190 cm tall.

What language(s) must you speak?

The official language of the project is English. However, you do not need to have a good level of English to take part in the selection process. You can apply in English, Spanish, Portuguese, French, German, Russian, Arabic, Mandarin Chinese, Korean, Indonesian or Japanese.

When will it happen and how long will it take?

Six teams of four will be chosen for training. They will train together until the launch in 2024. It takes seven months to get to Mars in an extremely challenging environment.

GRAMMAR
-ing and infinitive forms

A Complete the extracts with the correct form of the verbs in brackets. Then listen and check.

🔊 5.8

1 For centuries, man has been obsessed with the idea of _____ (*go*) to Mars.

2 I think it's important _____ (*advance*) science whenever the opportunity presents itself.

3 _____ (*be*) a scientist isn't enough.

4 I really appreciate _____ (*drink*) a good cup of coffee every morning.

5 I'll never forget _____ (*run*) across the Sahara Desert for seven days.

6 I'm going to Mars _____ (*be*) a part of history.

7 We have to learn _____ (*live*) independently of planet Earth.

8 Some people get really stressed when they forget _____ (*take*) their phone with them.

9 In space, all you can _____ (*hear*) is endless silence.

B SPEAK Work in pairs. Look at sentences 5 and 8 in Exercise A. What's the difference in meaning of the word *forget* in each of these sentences?

C WORK IT OUT Match the examples in Exercise A to the rules in the box.

-ing and infinitive forms

We use verb + -*ing*:

a after prepositions ___

b as the subject of a sentence ___

c after some verbs (e.g. *admit, appreciate, avoid, finish, give up, mind, suggest,* etc) ___

We use *to* + infinitive:

d after adjectives ___

e to talk about purpose ___

f after some verbs (e.g. *attempt, decide, expect, learn, manage, need, promise,* etc) ___

We use infinitive:

g after modal verbs ___

Some verbs can be followed by either verb + -*ing* or *to* + infinitive, but with a change of meaning (e.g. *forget, remember, try, go on,* etc)

h ___ / ___

D Go to the Grammar Hub on page XIV.

E PRACTISE Complete the sentences with the correct form of the verbs in the box.

> be do get have like
> plan produce work

1 _____ a positive attitude is the key to being a good team player.

2 It's important _____ everyone you work with.

3 One way of _____ more effective in a team is to become an active listener.

4 Never promise _____ more work than you can manage. You will let your team down.

5 Only teams with strong leaders can _____ good results.

6 Always remember _____ what you need to discuss in a team meeting, so you don't waste any time.

7 I'm worried about not _____ on with the other people in the team.

8 We need _____ together if we want to succeed.

F SPEAK Work in pairs. Do you agree with the sentences in Exercise E? Why/Why not?

⭕ SPEAKING HUB

A Go to the Communication Hub on page XXI.

B PRESENT Tell the class which candidates you chose, which you rejected and why.

○─ Talk about changes in your town or city
○─ Evaluate candidates and put together a team

▶ Reward or penalty?

COMPREHENSION

A Work in pairs. Look at the picture. Do you think cups like these are environmentally friendly? Why/Why not?

Glossary

disposable (adj) designed to be used once, then thrown away

B ▶ Watch a news report about an environmentally friendly scheme at a university. Choose the best summary (1 or 2).

1 The university found that a reward scheme had no meaningful effect on student behaviour. By adopting a penalty scheme instead, they were able to reduce the number of disposable cups sold every year.

2 The university found that a penalty scheme had no meaningful effect on student behaviour. By adopting a reward scheme instead, they were able to reduce the number of disposable cups sold every year.

C ▶ Watch the news report again and answer the questions.

1 How did the university originally try to encourage students to start using reusable cups?

2 What was the issue with the original scheme?

3 How did the university address this issue?

4 What else did the university do to encourage use of non-disposable cups?

5 Was the penalty scheme a success? Why/Why not?

6 How has the penalty scheme affected sales of hot drinks?

D Work in groups. Do you agree that you have to use penalties to meaningfully change behaviour? Why/Why not?

AUTHENTIC ENGLISH

A ▶ 01:33–01:41 Watch the last part of the report again and complete the extract.

Presenter: So this might work on a campus. That doesn't mean it's going to work on the high street, where people have a lot more choice.

Interviewee: _____ government were to legislate for it.

B Work in pairs. Read the extract again. Why does the speaker use a conditional? Which word does she stress? Why?

C Read the information in the box to check your answers to Exercise B.

Conditional counterarguments

In discussions, speakers sometimes use conditional structures to make a counterargument. These often begin with conjunctions and use words, phrases or ideas from the original argument. The stress is usually put on the modal verb to emphasise the contrast between the two ideas.

A: It's a nice idea, but just doesn't work in practice. Nobody wants to carry around a reusable cup everywhere they go.

B: But they might if coffee shops offered bigger discounts.

D Work in pairs. Take turns reading the arguments (1–3) and responding with a conditional.

1 Sadly, most people like the convenience of disposable water bottles. This isn't going to change anytime soon.

2 Social media isn't dangerous. It's just a fun way to stay in touch with old friends.

3 Electric cars are a great idea, but will never replace petrol vehicles on our roads.

SAM   MALCOLM   AMANDA   HARRY   EMILY

▶ A green suggestion

A Work in groups. Do you think where you work or study does enough to protect the environment? Why/Why not?

B ▶ Watch the video and answer the questions.

1 What eco-friendly change does Harry suggest?

2 Why does Amanda support this idea?

3 What is Sam's criticism of the idea?

SPEAKING SKILL

A Read the extract from the conversation. Why do you think Amanda finishes Harry's sentence?

Harry: People respond better to a penalty than a …

Amanda: … reward. It's what we do at my office.

B Read the information in the box and check your answers to Exercise A.

Taking the floor

In discussions, one speaker will often interrupt another so they can start speaking. This is called taking the floor. In the video, Sam interrupts Harry by saying [1]_____ and Malcolm interrupts Sam by saying [2]_____.

To keep the floor, we need to avoid interruption. In the video, Harry stops Sam from interrupting him by saying [3]_____.

We can also take the floor by agreeing or disagreeing with what someone has said.

Sam: Yes, well, I think we already do a fair bit to help the environment.

Harry: [4]_____ *we could do more?*

Amanda: And it does seem to have changed how people behave.

Harry: [5]_____. *People begin to feel that it's normal to have their own cup. It's not something that deserves a special reward.*

Sam: [6]_____ *we start penalising them.*

We can also show agreement or understanding by finishing someone's sentence, like Amanda does to Harry.

C ▶ Watch the video again. Complete the box with examples from the conversation.

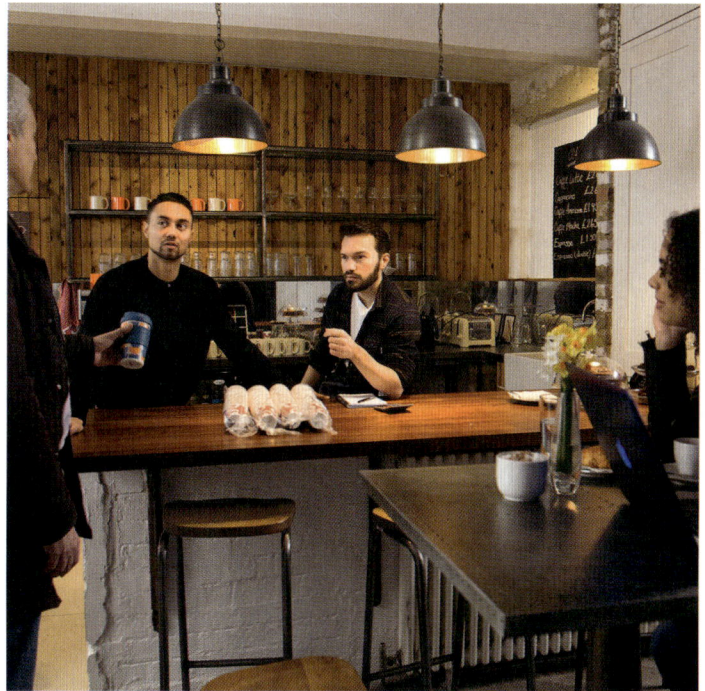

D Work in groups. Discuss one of the following topics using strategies from the box to take or keep the floor.

- recycling
- wind farms
- solar panels
- electric cars
- plastic packaging
- food waste

SPEAKING HUB

A **PREPARE** Work in groups. Write a list of five ways you could be more environmentally friendly in the following areas:

- travel and transport
- recycling
- saving water
- eating smart
- reducing and reusing
- clothing

B **PLAN** Rank the points in Exercise A in order of importance. Try to reach an agreement in the group.

A: I really think recycling plastics is a top priority. We should all carry refillable water bottles with us.

B: Really? But surely people wouldn't want to carry a water bottle everywhere.

A: But they might if governments made plastic bottles expensive and provided lots of places where we can refill our bottles.

C **PRESENT** Present your list to the class. Explain your reasoning.

◯– **Discuss ways to help the environment**

➤ Turn to page XXVIII to learn how to write a problem solution article.

VOCABULARY

A Complete the definitions with the words in the box.

> insulation   smart meter   solar panel
> thermostat   water butt   wind turbine

1 _____ a large container used to collect rain for watering plants

2 _____ a large machine like a windmill used for producing electricity using the wind

3 _____ material used to prevent heat, cold, noise, etc from passing through something

4 _____ an electronic device used to record how much electricity is used

5 _____ a piece of equipment that uses energy from the sun to create electricity

6 _____ a piece of equipment that controls the temperature in a building

B Complete the sentences with the words in the box.

> housing   residential   rural   slums   suburbs   urban

1 They are building a new _____ area near me with over 2000 new homes.

2 The cost of _____ has increased by nearly 20% in the last year.

3 I don't really like living in the _____. It's too far from the centre and there isn't much to do.

4 In countries such as Germany and England, nearly 80% of the population live in _____ areas.

5 Because of high unemployment, many people leave _____ areas and move to cities to look for work.

6 In many _____, many thousands of people have to share just one toilet.

C Complete the article with the correct form on the words in brackets.

Simple ways to be more environmentally friendly

Climate change is a threat to all of us. You can help tackle this issue by making some of the following changes:

1 Buy a reusable bottle

Many plastics are used just once and can't be
1 _____ (recycle). Many people believe single-use plastics are 2 _____ (necessary) and should be banned. To help prevent plastic pollution, take a reusable water bottle with you instead of buying a plastic one.

2 Cycle to work

Air pollution is also a major problem, particularly in
3 _____ (crowded) cities. Campaigners would like heavily polluting vehicles to be made
4 _____ (legal). In the past, a lot of cycle paths were 5 _____ (standard) but there has been a lot of recent investment in building new cycle paths. Cycling to work is a great way to help reduce pollution while also getting some exercise!

GRAMMAR

A Complete the sentences with the correct passive form of the verbs in the box.

> build   film   finish   hold   inform   left

1 Parts of *Star Wars: The Last Jedi* _____ in the salt plains of Bolivia.

2 An emergency meeting _____ to discuss possible responses.

3 The public _____ about the potential risk and are advised to avoid the area.

4 The house, which was the family home of the Harrogates, _____ in 1858.

5 As they pulled into their drive, they noticed that the window _____ open.

6 The new shopping centre was scheduled to be completed by now but it _____ until next May.

B Complete the sentences with the correct form of the words in brackets.

1 A: Can you give me a lift tonight?

   B: No, sorry. I _____ (my car / service) at the moment.

2 A: _____ (you / your shower / fix)?

   B: Not yet. Someone's coming to look at it tomorrow.

3 A: Have you seen Emily?

   B: Yes, she's _____ (nails / paint).

4 A: Why are they eating out so much?

   B: They are _____ (kitchen / installed) this week.

5 A: Everyone on TV has such white teeth!

   B: I know. Actually, I'm thinking about _____ _____ (teeth / whiten).

C Choose the correct options (a or b) to complete the sentences.

1 Chris has offered ___ me with the project I'm doing about homelessness.

   a to help   b helping

2 Mark has been in touch. Did you remember ___ him an email?

   a to send   b sending

3 I don't want ___ to work today, but I have so much to do.

   a to go   b going

4 Lucy texted. They're aiming ___ to the party for eight.

   a to get   b getting

5 Our kids miss ___ in Madrid and wish we could move back.

   a to live   b living

6 These videos on YouTube are great to help you learn how ___ the guitar.

   a to play   b playing

Endmatter Contents

Grammar Hub

1.1 Question forms

Questions with *be, have* and *do*

- We often use the auxiliary verbs *be, have* and *do* to form questions. These come before the main verb.

Question word	Auxiliary	Subject	Main verb	
	Is	he	coming	this weekend?
	Have	you	seen	her?
When	did	they	move	in?

Subject questions

- When the question word (*who, what,* etc) is the subject, we don't use an auxiliary.

Question word	Main verb	
What	happened	to you?
How	are	you?

Indirect questions

- Indirect questions begin with phrases such as *Can you tell me …?* After the phrase, we use the same word order as a sentence, not a question.

  Do you think it will rain? NOT ~~Do you think will it rain?~~

  Can you tell me where you live? NOT ~~Can you tell me where do you live?~~

Questions ending in a preposition

- When a question word is the object of a preposition, the preposition usually comes at the end of the sentence.

  Who did you brother live with?
  What did you use it for?

Questions with negative auxiliaries

- When we ask negative *wh-* questions, we use the auxiliary verb, even in subject questions. Negative *wh-* questions can be used to confirm something you believe to be true, to express an opinion in a more formal manner or to focus on a smaller number of answers.

  *OK, who **doesn't** want pizza? (= I think most people **will** want pizza)*

1.2 Tense review

Present simple	**He enjoys** parties.
Present continuous	**I'm watching** the news.
Past simple	**He got up** early this morning.
Past continuous	**I was walking** the dog.
Present perfect simple	**I've lived** here for 12 years.
Past perfect simple	**I'd seen** the film several times.

- We use the present simple to talk about general truths or actions that always/usually/never happen as part of our daily routines.
- We use the present continuous for things that are happening now or around now.
- We use the past simple to talk about past states or completed actions in the past.
- We use the past continuous to describe the background to a story or something that was in progress at a particular time in the past. We also use it with the past simple to describe an action that was interrupted.

  We were driving home when we had an unexpected phone call.

- We use the present perfect simple to talk about a state or action that started in the past and is still happening now. We also use it to announce news.
- We use the past perfect simple to talk about a past action that occurred before another past action. This tense is often used with the past simple.
- With the negative and question forms of these tenses, we use an auxiliary verb (*be, do* or *have*, depending on the tense).

  She doesn't feel well.
  It didn't cost a lot.
  I haven't finished yet.
  Had they been there before?

Be careful!

- Certain time words and expressions, such as *now, at the moment, just, already, recently, every day,* etc, help us to identify which tense we need to use.

  *I was travelling across the country **at the time**.*
  *I have **just** finished the last series on Netflix.*
  *Actually, I saw him at the gym **yesterday**.*

1.1 Question forms

A Correct the mistakes in each question.

1 Does he lives near here?
2 What she has done to her hair?
3 Where you work?
4 Which is team winning?
5 Haven't you already be on holiday?
6 Who with do you live?
7 When he told you that?
8 What was happened next?

B Rewrite the direct questions as indirect questions.

1 Where did you get your information?
Can you tell me _____?
2 Is it going to snow later, do you think?
Do you think _____?
3 What do you think of the new recycling laws?
Can I ask you _____?
4 Where does Alejandro come from?
Do you know _____?
5 Has the post arrived yet?
Could you see if _____?

C Complete the questions in the interview.

Interviewer: Where ¹_____ ?
Mia: I'm from Seattle, Washington.
Interviewer: How long ²_____ ?
Mia: I've been here for about five years now.
Interviewer: Who ³_____ ?
Mia: With friends, but I'm looking to find a flat of my own.
Interviewer: So when ⁴_____ ?
Mia: I guess I decided to become an actor when I was about five!
Interviewer: What ⁵_____ ?
Mia: I don't have much free time, but when I am free, I like spending time with friends and family.
Interviewer: Do you think ⁶_____ ?
Mia: Oh yes. I think I'll always be an actor. I can't imagine doing anything else!

➤ Go back to page 5.

1.2 Tense review

A Choose the correct options to complete the sentences.

1 I *am* / *was* watching television when I started to feel ill.
2 Joanna was ashamed because she *has* / *had* done something wrong.
3 I *am never feeling* / *have never felt* relaxed around him – I don't know why.
4 We *were taking* / *had taken* the wrong turning and were now completely lost.
5 I'm pretty sure I *met* / *have met* you at Jenna's party last year.
6 While I *was walking* / *had walked* home, I slipped on some ice and broke my ankle.
7 I *live* / *have lived* here for about a year and a half now.
8 James *studies* / *is studying* French at Oxford next year.

B Complete the sentences with the correct form of the verb in brackets.

1 Jochen is an anxious person who _____ _____ (not like) doing new things.
2 It wasn't awkward at the party because I _____ _____ (already meet) everyone there.
3 The question is: why was Tom there – who _____ _____ (wait) for?
4 I've got some really exciting news – I _____ _____ (get) a new job!
5 We _____ (work) on a secret project these days.
6 Tell me about yourself. How long _____ _____ (work) for this company?

C Complete the sentences with the correct form of the verbs in the box. Use contractions where possible.

| forget | have | know | meet |
| snow | think | walk | work |

1 It _____ heavily and I wasn't wearing a winter coat.
2 She _____ for the company for nearly five years now.
3 It's difficult because he _____ many people in the area.
4 We _____ much money back then, but we were happy.
5 I knew I _____ her before, but I couldn't figure out where.
6 I _____ about starting my own company.
7 I _____ down the road in the sunshine when out of nowhere, it suddenly started pouring with rain.
8 She only realised she _____ her passport when she got to the airport.

➤ Go back to page 7.

Grammar Hub

2.1 Present perfect simple and present perfect continuous

	Positive	Negative	Question
Present perfect simple	**He's improved** his fitness level.	**They haven't finished** their meeting yet.	**Have you lost** weight?
Present perfect continuous	**I've been trying** to give up sugar.	**She hasn't been sleeping** very well.	**Have you been avoiding** me?

- We use the present perfect simple for finished actions with a present effect, and the present perfect continuous for unfinished actions.

  I've read that book before, actually.
  (= I finished the book.)
  I've been reading a great book recently.
  (= I started it and I'm still reading it.)

- We use the present perfect simple to emphasise the result of an action, and the present perfect continuous to emphasise the action itself.

  I've cleaned the bathroom.
  (emphasising the result: the bathroom's now clean)
  I've been cleaning the bathroom all morning.
  (emphasising the action: the cleaning)

- We use the present perfect simple to suggest that something is permanent and the present perfect continuous to suggest that something is temporary.

  I've lived here my whole life. (= long-term/permanent)
  I've been living here while I look for a new flat.
  (= short-term/temporary)

- We use the present perfect simple to say how often something has happened and the present perfect continuous to say how long something has been happening.

  I've been to the gym every day this week. (= number of times)
  I've been going to the gym for the past two months.
  (= length of time)

> **Be careful!**
>
> - We don't usually use state verbs such as *be, have, know* and *seem* in the present perfect continuous.
>
>   *She's had short hair for several months now.*
>   *NOT She's been having short hair for several months now.*

2.2 *used to / would / be used to / get used to*

	Positive	Negative	Question
used to	**I used to work** in a hotel.	**He didn't use to get** so stressed.	**Did she use to have** long hair?
would	**They would take** the bus to work.	**She wouldn't have** anything for breakfast.	**Would he often come** home late?
be used to	**He's used to getting** up early.	**I'm not used to eating** such spicy food.	**Are you used to driving** on the left now?
get used to	**He** soon **got used to wearing** glasses.	**I haven't got used to** the cold weather.	**Are you getting used to living** in the countryside?

- We use *used to* + infinitive to talk about past habits, repeated actions and states or situations that have changed.

  I used to get up really early at the weekend.
  He didn't use to have a beard.

- We also use *would* + infinitive to talk about past habits and repeated actions.

  The children would spend hours playing in the garden.

- We use *be used to* + verb + *-ing/*noun to talk about a situation which is now normal or familiar. We use the negative form to talk about a situation which is new or strange.

  I'm used to living on my own.
  I'm not used to the cold weather.

- We use *get used to* + verb + *-ing/*noun to talk about a situation which is becoming more familiar.

  I'm getting used to working in an office.
  I haven't got used to the food yet.

> **Be careful!**
>
> - We cannot use *would* to talk about past states.
>   *They used to live in London. NOT They would live in London.*

2.1 Present perfect simple and present perfect continuous

A Choose the correct options to complete the conversations.

1 **A:** How long have you *known / been knowing* Emily?

   B: Er, about five years now, I think.

2 **A:** Did you tell everyone about the change of venue?

   B: I think so. Oh no! I've just *realised / been realising* that I forgot to tell Piotr!

3 **A:** How's your essay going?

   B: I've *planned / been planning* it for the past three hours so I'm nearly ready to start writing.

4 **A:** Who'll be there this evening?

   B: Just me and my sister. She's *stayed / been staying* with me while her flat's redecorated.

5 **A:** I saw Toby in town today.

   B: Yes, his boss has *given / been giving* him a week off work.

6 **A:** So, what have you been up to?

   B: I've been *working / worked* on a new book. I should finish it by the end of the year.

B Complete the sentences with the present perfect simple or continuous form of the verbs in the box. Add pronouns if necessary.

| avoid be decide do find know |
| leave notice only go out think use wait |

1 They _____ about moving house now that their son _____ home.

2 Ren _____ the new shampoo for six months and she _____ a big improvement in her hair.

3 Lucia _____ to quit her job because she _____ it more and more stressful over the last few months.

4 Why _____ me? _____ something to upset you?

5 I _____ Farid for years, but we _____ for a few weeks!

6 I _____ for you for hours! Where _____ all this time?

C Use the prompts to write sentences in the present perfect simple or present perfect continuous.

1 Kim / not work / here for long, so she / not met / all of her colleagues yet

   _____.

2 I think Jamila and Kalid / already / send out / the invitations

   _____.

3 I'm afraid I / not tidy / the living room yet as I just / not have / time

   _____.

4 Jimmy / drive / for hours, so he must / be / exhausted

   _____.

5 I / know / about this for a long time

   _____.

6 How long / it / be / since you / quit / your job

   _____?

7 You / visit / this museum before

   _____?

8 We / eat / vegan food for two months now

   _____.

➤ Go back to page 17.

2.2 used to / would / be used to / get used to

A Choose the correct options to complete the sentences.

1 People *didn't use to / wouldn't* be able to look everything up on Google.

2 Sofia is slowly *used / getting used* to living back home with her parents.

3 *Did you use to / Would you* have a smartphone when you were younger?

4 *I'm still not used / I didn't use* to having short hair!

5 The children usually *got used / used* to spend their pocket money on sweets.

6 Jakob *got / was* used to wearing glasses fairly quickly.

7 *Were you / Have you got* used to the new software yet?

8 As a child, Milo *would / was used to* become demotivated very easily.

B Complete the text messages with the correct form of *used to*, *be used to* and *get used to*.

How's the new job going? Have you 1_____ the commute yet?

Not really. It 2_____ take about 20 minutes to get to work. Now it takes over an hour!

I know the feeling! I 3_____ having a long drive to work – I've been doing it for a while now – but I still 4_____ getting up so early!

It's horrible, isn't it? I 5_____ get up at half past seven. These days, that's when I have to leave the house. And I'm still 6_____ getting home so late, either.

➤ Go back to page 19.

3.1 Narrative tenses

	Positive	Negative	Question
Past simple	**The rescue team found** Jose and **carried** him to safety.	Unfortunately, **the rescue team didn't see** the survivors.	So what **did you do** next?
Past continuous	At the time, **most of us were trying** to get some sleep.	**I wasn't looking forward to** the journey.	What **were you doing** when the storm hit?
Past perfect simple	They returned to find that **the tornado had destroyed** their house.	They suddenly realised that **the helicopter hadn't seen** their signal.	**Had you been** in that kind of situation before?
Past perfect continuous	**She'd been swimming** for hours by the time she was rescued.	Although **they hadn't been driving** long, everyone was exhausted.	How long **had you been climbing** for?

- We use the past simple for completed actions that are the main events in a story.

  After some hours alone in the wood, Wei ate his last chocolate bar.

- We use the past continuous (*was/were* + verb + *-ing*) to describe:

  a actions in progress at a particular point in a story.
  He was charging his phone at the time.

  b longer actions or situations that are interrupted by a shorter action.
  They weren't wearing life jackets when the boat capsized. NOT They didn't wear life jackets when the boat capsized.

  c the general background of a story.
  The skies were getting dark, the winds were picking up and the passengers were beginning to worry.

- We use the past perfect simple (*had* + past participle) to describe past actions or situations that happened before one of the main events in the story, or before the story began.

  A lot of insects had bitten Francesco before he decided to use the insect repellent.

- We use the past perfect continuous (*had* + *been* + verb + *-ing*) to describe longer actions or situations that started before one of the main events and have continued up to that point.

  We'd been waiting for hours before we were rescued.

Be careful!

- We often use the past continuous after *while* and *as*.

  While she was standing by the side of the road, a car with dark windows pulled up.

- We can often use either the past simple or past perfect simple after *as soon as* and *by the time*.

  By the time I'd realised what was happening, Jilly had left.

3.2 Alternatives to *if* in conditionals

- We use *unless* to mean *if … not*.

  Generally, bears won't attack you unless they think you're a threat. (= They won't attack you if they don't think you're a threat.)

  Unless this weather improves, we'll be stuck in the camp all day. (= If the weather doesn't improve, we'll be stuck in the camp all day.)

- We use *provided (that)* and *as long as* to mean *only if*.

  They should be back soon provided (that) they don't take a wrong turn. (= They should be back soon, but only if they don't take a wrong turn.)

  As long as you stay on the path, you won't get lost. (= You won't get lost, but only if you stay on the path.)

- We use *in case* to talk about doing something now to prepare for a possible future situation.

  I'll take a waterproof jacket in case it starts raining. (= because it's possible it will start raining)

  She's going to stay in a safe spot in case she encounters a bear. (= because it's possible that she will encounter a bear)

- We use *as soon as* to mean *in the shortest possible time / immediately*.

  I'll call you as soon as I hear anything. (= I'll call you immediately after I hear something.)

Be careful!

- Even though we're talking about the future, we use a present tense after future time clauses.

  We'll leave as soon as the storm clears. NOT We'll leave as soon as the storm will clear.

  Elephants won't attack you unless you run towards them. NOT Elephants won't attack you unless you will run towards them.

3.1 Narrative tenses

A Choose the correct options (a, b or c) to complete the sentences.

1 Nozomi ___ her bike when it started raining.

   a was riding   **b** rode   **c** had ridden

2 We ___ down the side of the mountain when our rope snapped.

   a had climbed   **b** were climbing   **c** climbed

3 The ship ___ into a rock, but no one was hurt.

   a had crashed   **b** was crashing   **c** crashed

4 I ___ my tent when suddenly I heard a strange noise in the forest behind me.

   a packed away   **b** had packed away   **c** was packing away

5 The next day, they saw that the hurricane ___ the house off the ground!

   a was lifting   **b** had lifted   **c** lifted

6 When the wave hit the ship, everyone ___ to panic.

   a had started   **b** started   **c** was starting

7 The sun ___ and the conditions were perfect for hiking.

   a was shining   **b** had shone   **c** shone

8 We ___ for eight hours when the captain told us to prepare for an emergency landing.

   a were flying   **b** had been flying   **c** flew

B Complete the story with the correct form of the verbs in the box.

> approach carry faint fall fly
> happen serve take off

Something strange [1]_____ the last time I was on a plane. I [2]_____ to Moscow on a business trip. We [3]_____ from Frankfurt about an hour before, and the cabin crew [4]_____ drinks. Suddenly, one of the cabin crew near me just [5]_____ to the floor. We didn't know if he [6]_____ or had had a heart attack. Other members of the crew rushed to help him, and [7]_____ him to the back of the plane. Just as we [8]_____ Moscow, the captain made an announcement, telling us that the crew member was fine. I was very relieved.

➤ Go back to page 27.

3.2 Alternatives to *if* in conditionals

A Choose the correct options to complete the sentences.

1 They'll survive in the woods *provided / unless* they have enough food.

2 *Unless / Provided* we leave right now, we'll never make it back to the camp before dark.

3 I'll let you start the fire *as soon as / as long as* you know what you're doing!

4 Do Yoon is bringing extra water *as long as / in case* we run out.

5 Let's give Margie a call *as soon as / as long as* we reach the cabin.

6 *As long as / Unless* you have a better suggestion, let's have pizza tonight.

7 I wrote their number on a piece of paper *in case / unless* my phone battery dies.

8 We'll go fishing at the river tomorrow *as long as / in case* it doesn't rain.

B Are these sentences correct or incorrect? Rewrite the incorrect sentences.

1 We'll call the police as soon as we will get to safety.

2 I'll cancel the trip unless Tara will decide to go with me.

3 You can go to the party provided you're back home by 11 o'clock.

4 Unless the taxi doesn't come soon, we're going to be late.

5 Take some seasickness pills with you in case the sea will be rough.

6 Will you call me as soon as you arrive at the airport?

7 He'll sleep on the ship as long as the weather won't be too bad.

8 I'll take the risk provided you think it's worth it.

C Match the numbers (1–10) with the letters (a–j) to make conditional sentences.

1 Provided you don't make any sudden movements, ___

2 She won't use her credit card ___

3 You won't get into trouble ___

4 Astrid should give David the money now ___

5 As long as you promise to pay him back, ___

6 I'll come with you as ___

7 Unless we stay late, ___

8 I'm going to take a map with me ___

9 Provided that we stay somewhere cheap, ___

10 I'll buy the tickets ___

  a provided you tell the truth.

  b I'd love to come with you to Paris.

  c in case she doesn't see him later.

  d in case we get lost.

  e we'll never get all this work done on time.

  f he said that he would get the food for the party.

  g unless it's an emergency.

  h as soon as they're available online.

  i you should be perfectly safe.

  j long as we make sure we're back home by five.

➤ Go back to page 31.

Grammar Hub

4.1 Future forms

- We use *will* + infinitive:

  a for decisions made at the moment of speaking (including promises, offers, plans and requests).
  That's a good idea – I'll call him now.
  That looks heavy – I'll carry it for you.

  b to make predictions based on personal opinions or feelings (often with adverbs like *definitely, certainly, possibly,* etc to show how sure we are).
  Tom will definitely be late – he always is!
  Mum won't like that film. It's not her sort of thing.

- We use *be going to* + infinitive:

  a to talk about general intentions and plans made before the moment of speaking.
  I'm going to look for a new job.

  b to make predictions based on present evidence.
  The traffic's not moving – we're going to be late!

- We use the present simple to talk about a timetabled or scheduled event.
  Our flight leaves at 8.30 am on Monday.
  My job interview is tomorrow morning.

- We use the present continuous to talk about future arrangements and fixed plans.
  We're staying in a hostel for the first three nights. (= We've already booked the hostel.)
  I'm meeting Sarah at 7.30 pm outside the restaurant. (= We've already arranged to meet at that time and place.)

4.2 Future perfect simple, future continuous and future perfect continuous

	Positive	Negative	Question
Future perfect simple	**The film will have started** by the time we get there!	**I won't have finished** the report by tomorrow morning.	**Will you have left** by then?
Future continuous	**I'll be seeing** her on Monday, so I could ask her then.	**We won't be using** driverless cars for at least another 50 years.	So, what **will you be doing** this time tomorrow?
Future perfect continuous	In 2041, **we'll have been using** the internet for 50 years.	**I won't have been running** long enough to try a half-marathon in July.	How long **will you have been travelling** by then?

- We use the future perfect simple (*will* + *have* + past participle) to talk about something that will be finished before a specific time in the future.
  By 2050, we will have greatly improved the air quality in our cities.

- We use the future continuous (*will* + *be* + verb + *-ing*) to talk about an action that will be in progress at a specific time in the future.
  Hopefully, I'll be working in New York by then.

- We use the future perfect continuous (*will* + *have* + *been* + verb + *-ing*) to talk about an action or situation that will continue up to a specific time in the future.
  By 9th July, I'll have been working here for seven years.

- Certain time words and expressions are used with these tenses.
  In 50 years' time, we'll have stopped using petrol vehicles.
  This time next year, we'll be studying in France.
  By 2020, we will have been living together for 20 years.

Be careful!

- Do not confuse these three tenses. The future perfect simple is used for *completed* actions in the future, while the future continuous is used for actions *in progress* at a certain point in the future. The future perfect continuous refers to how long something will be in progress before a certain point in the future.
  I will have paid for my house by 2025. NOT I will be paying for my house by 2025.
  I will be living in the USA in five years' time. NOT I will have lived in the USA in five years' time.
  I will have been living here for 15 years in 2025. NOT I will be living here for 15 years in 2025.

4.1 Future forms

A Choose the correct options to complete the sentences.

1 I *have / am having* French lessons every Monday night at seven o'clock.

2 *I'm meeting / I will meet* friends for lunch on Sunday.

3 *We'll probably / We're going to* move house this year but I'm not certain.

4 It looks like they *will / are going to* win. They're 4–0 up with only a minute left to play.

5 I think the plane *arrives / will arrive* late.

6 I've had enough of this job! I'm *looking for / going to look for* a new one.

B Complete the post with the correct future form of the verbs in brackets. Use contractions where possible.

Emily | 20 mins ago

So, big news! I've got a place at NYU to study Performing Arts, so [1] _____ (*I / move*) to New York in September! Apparently, I can stay in the residence halls near the main campus, but I've decided [2] _____ (*I / look for*) my own apartment. Wouldn't that be amazing? [3] _____ (*I / definitely / have to*) get a job to pay the rent, but it would be nice to have my own space. I've never lived abroad before, so [4] _____ (*it / be*) difficult to be so far away from my family. But everyone's been so supportive! Anyway, my [5] _____ (*flight / leave*) early on 28th August so if any of you want to meet up before then, just send me a message and [6] _____ (*I / get back*) to you.

C Are these sentences correct or incorrect? Rewrite the incorrect sentences.

1 Having my young nephews to stay in the house next week is being exhausting!

2 The lecture starts at seven tomorrow evening, not eight.

3 I'm afraid that we aren't going on a cruise this year.

4 I'm feeling really tired, so I think I go to bed soon.

5 Are you starting looking for a job anytime soon?

6 We meet Andy and Karim for lunch on 12th May.

7 I probably won't get there until at least half past ten.

8 I'm helping you do the dishes, if you like.

➤ Go back to page 39.

4.2 Future perfect simple, future continuous and future perfect continuous

A Choose the correct options (a, b or c) to complete the sentences.

1 It's a nine-hour flight. My plane leaves at 9 am, so at 11 am, I ___.
   a 'll be flying over the Atlantic   **b** 'll have landed in New York

2 Do you really think you'll ___ at the same company in ten years' time?
   a have worked   **b** be working

3 This time next year, he ___ for Real Madrid for ten years.
   a 'll have been playing   **b** 'll be playing

4 Do you think you ___ English in five years' time?
   a 'll have studied   **b** 'll still be studying

5 Is it possible that they ___ the use of fossil fuels by the time our children grow up?
   a 'll be banning   **b** 'll have banned

6 What will you ___ at three tomorrow? If you're free, let's meet up for a chat.
   a have done   **b** be doing

7 Next Sunday, I ___ here for two years.
   a 'll have been living   **b** 'll be living

B Complete the sentences with the future perfect simple, future continuous or future perfect continuous form of the verb in brackets.

1 _____ (*you / finish*) your studies by the end of the year?

2 I started learning English over four years ago, so in December, I will _____ (*study*) it for exactly five years.

3 Within the next ten years, robots _____ (*take*) over a lot of tasks.

4 What kind of world do you think we _____ (*live*) in 50 years from now?

5 If the sea level rises, these cities _____ (*completely / disappear*) in 100 years.

6 In June of next year, you _____ (*work*) here for five years.

➤ Go back to page 43.

Grammar Hub

5.1 The passive; causative *have* and *get*

The passive

Present simple	**Most of the children are taken** to school by bus.
Present continuous	**We aren't being told** the truth about the extent of the damage.
Present perfect	**Has the amount of waste been reduced**?
Past simple	**The deer was killed** by a hunter.
Past continuous	**The forest was being cut down** by construction companies.
Past perfect	**The law hadn't been changed** for years.
will	How **will the park be affected** by the road?
Modals	**The plans can't be changed** now.
to + infinitive	**This area** is too polluted **to be used**.

- We use the passive (*be* + past participle) when:

  a we don't know who or what caused something to happen, or when this is not important.

  A fire was started in a small area of woodland near the park entrance. (= We don't know who started the fire.)

  b we want to focus on the action, not what caused it.

  Huge amounts of CO$_2$ are being added to the atmosphere every year. (= The focus here is the CO$_2$ – we aren't really interested in who or what is adding it.)

  c it's obvious from the context who or what caused the action.

  The law has already been changed in many countries. (= It's obvious that it was the government of these countries that changed the law.)

> **Be careful!**
>
> - When we say who performed an action, we use *by*.
>
> *The research is being carried out **by** the US National Park Service.*

Causative *have* and *get*

Positive	Negative	Question
I'm having solar panels **installed**.	**We haven't had** the windows **replaced** yet.	**Are you getting** a smart meter **fitted**?

- We use causative *have* and *get* (*have/get* + object + past participle) to say that someone does something for us – often for tasks we can't or don't know how to do ourselves.

  My parents are having a new garage built.

- We can also use causative *have* to describe something unwelcome or negative happening to us.

  I've had my bike stolen twice this month!

5.2 *-ing* and infinitive forms

- We use verb + *-ing*:

  a after prepositions.

  *I'm thinking **about moving** to another company.*

  b as the subject or object of a sentence.

  ***Travelling** around South Korea was fantastic.*

  c after certain verbs (e.g. *admit, avoid, finish, mind*, etc).

  *I **don't mind living** in the suburbs.*

- We use *to* + infinitive:

  a after adjectives.

  *It can be **difficult to find** your dream job.*

  b to talk about purpose (i.e. what someone wants to achieve).

  *I came to London **to improve** my level of English. (= This explains why I came here.)*

  c after certain verbs (e.g. *agree, attempt, decide, hope, manage, promise*, etc).

  *Has the City Council **agreed to build** more housing?*

- The infinitive is always used after modal verbs (e.g. *may, might, would*, etc) and after the verbs let and make.

  *I think I **would make** an excellent candidate for the Mars One programme.*

> **Be careful!**
>
> - Some verbs can be followed by either verb + *-ing* or *to* + infinitive, but with a change of meaning (e.g. *forget, go on, regret, remember, stop, try*, etc)
>
> *I'll never forget **waking up** in Tokyo for the first time. (= I have a memory of this.)*
>
> *My daughter never forgets **to phone** me on my birthday. (= She doesn't forget to do this.)*

5.1 The passive

A Rewrite the sentences in the passive, omitting the agent where appropriate.

1 Millions of people watch the World Cup final.

The World Cup final _____.

2 High CO_2 levels are causing global warming.

Global warming _____.

3 We've recently fitted our loft with insulation.

Our loft _____.

4 When did they announce the winners of the competition?

When _____?

5 The council is going to cut down the tree.

The tree _____.

6 An electrician needs to install this kind of shower.

This kind of shower needs _____.

B Complete the paragraph with the correct passive form of the verbs in the box.

| collect | confirm | deliver | inform | pack | print | send | take |

ONLINE SHOPPING
behind the scenes

Someone has just ordered some new clothes online. But what happens behind the scenes before the items can [1]_____ to their door? Once the credit card payment [2]_____, an order confirmation email [3]_____ automatically to the customer, and the people in the packing team [4]_____ of the order. One of them then collects the items from the warehouse in order for them to [5]_____. Next the shipping label [6]_____, and either the package [7]_____ by a courier or it [8]_____ to the post office for its journey to the customer.

➤ Go back to page 51.

Causative *have* and *get*

Put the words in the correct order to make sentences with causative *have* and *get*.

1 getting / I'm / the / locally. / posters / printed

_____

2 to / bike / going / get / repaired? / your / When / you / are

_____

3 the heating system / at / a plumber. / by / need / get / looked / I / to

_____

4 has / her / hair / wife / six weeks. / My / every / cut

_____

5 teeth / tomorrow. / having / checked / are / their / The dogs

_____

6 new / expensive? / Will / very / having / installed / a / kitchen / be

_____

7 having / After / better. / painted, / house / it / much / so / looked / our

_____

8 had / their / neighbours / house / night. / into / Our / last / broken

_____

➤ Go back to page 53.

5.2 *-ing* and infinitive forms

A Choose the correct options to complete the sentences.

1 We agreed *to do* / *doing* our project on the topic of megacities.

2 He really appreciates *to be* / *being* able to travel so much.

3 The council has passed a law *protect* / *to protect* old buildings.

4 They let us *walk* / *to walk* around the museum at night.

5 Did you manage *to book* / *booking* the tickets for the tour?

6 They made her *completing* / *complete* an online application form.

7 I'm really looking forward to *having* / *have* a few days off work.

8 *Invite* / *Inviting* so many people to dinner really wasn't a good idea.

B Are these sentences correct or incorrect? Rewrite the incorrect sentences.

1 After a poor start, he went on winning the match in the end.

2 I fondly remember to visit Abu Dhabi when I was about your age.

3 I forgot to tell you that I entered that photography competition.

4 We regret informing passengers that the flight to Seoul has been delayed.

5 Stop to talk about your holidays all the time – it's making me jealous!

6 We tried to book tickets for the Coffee Museum in Dubai but it was closed.

➤ Go back to page 57.

Vocabulary Hub

1.1 Feelings

A Label the pictures (1–8) with the adjectives in the box.

> awkward   devastated   disgusted   frustrated   furious   overwhelmed   relieved   stunned

1 _____

2 _____

3 _____

4 _____

5 _____

6 _____

7 _____

8 _____

B Choose the correct options (a, b or c) to complete the sentences.

1 I was so ___ I had to leave the room. I didn't want a serious argument.

  a furious   **b** stunned   **c** relieved

2 I was ___ when I lost my ring. My grandma had given it to me when I was little.

  a disgusted   **b** relieved   **c** devastated

3 I was ___ by the lack of help. How could people just watch and do nothing?

  a furious   **b** overwhelmed   **c** disgusted

4 To be honest I felt a bit ___. We hadn't parted on good terms.

  a awkward   **b** relieved   **c** frustrated

5 I'm so ___ we didn't miss our flight! I don't know what we would have done if we had.

  a furious   **b** stunned   **c** relieved

6 I think my grandad gets pretty ___ that he can't do everything for himself anymore.

  a furious   **b** overwhelmed   **c** frustrated

➤ Go back to page 3.

1.2 Personality adjectives

A Match the personality adjectives (1–8) with the definitions (a–h).

1 I loved his talk. He was so **passionate** about what he was saying. ___
2 You're always so **optimistic**. I wish I could be more positive like you. ___
3 Don't be so **pessimistic**. It might not be so bad. ___
4 She's really **ambitious**. She wants to own her own company in two years' time. ___
5 Try not to be so **sensitive**. I'm sure he didn't mean to upset you. ___
6 He's really **naïve**. He'll believe anything you tell him. ___
7 She was **determined** to finish the race, even though she was injured. ___
8 You need to be really **flexible** to work here. They are always changing our jobs. ___

a thinking that the worst thing will happen in every situation
b likely to become upset quickly
c lacking experience in life and too ready to trust or believe in others
d showing or expressing strong beliefs, interest or enthusiasm
e able to make changes or deal with a situation that is changing
f being hopeful about the future and expecting that good things will happen
g not willing to let anything prevent you from doing what you have decided to do
h wanting to be successful, rich, famous, etc

B Complete the job adverts with adjectives from Exercise A. Use each adjective only once.

Salesperson

We are looking for a new salesperson to join our team. We need hard-working people who can reach our high targets. You should be ¹_____, with big plans for your career. We work long hours, including weekends, so you will need to be ²_____ about when you work. Some of our products are challenging to sell so you will need to remain positive and not develop a ³_____ attitude.

CHARITY WORKER

Is someone being ⁴_____ and unrealistic when they think they can change the world? We don't think so! We welcome ⁵_____ people who believe that we really can make a difference and that even small things can have a huge impact. We are looking to hire someone who can be ⁶_____ towards people's needs and who is ⁷_____ to help make other people's lives better. If you are ⁸_____ about making the world a better place, then this could be the job for you!

➤ Go back to page 9.

2.1 Health and fitness

Complete the sentences with the words and phrases in the box.

| level of fitness   life expectancy   mental health   physical   processed foods   reduce the risk   slow the ageing process |

1 To remain healthy, adults should do at least 150 minutes of moderate _____ activity, like cycling, every week.
2 The average _____ for women is typically two or three years longer than for men.
3 Some _____ contain high levels of salt, fat and sugar.
4 Eating a balanced diet and doing regular exercise may help _____.
5 A healthy diet and regular exercise can both significantly _____ of high blood pressure.
6 Improving your _____ can help to fight various heart-related diseases.
7 Surprisingly, exercise can also be good for your _____ as it reduces levels of stress and anxiety.

➤ Go back to page 14.

Vocabulary Hub

3.1 Descriptive verbs

Complete the sentences (1–8) with the verbs in the box.

crackling creaked growling rumbled screeched slamming smashed whirring

1 It was pouring with rain and thunder _____ in the distance.

2 The tyres _____ as she tried to stop the car in time.

3 The floorboards _____ under his weight as he tried to tiptoe down the stairs.

4 They sat around the _____ fire, wondering what to do next.
➤ Go back to page 29.

5 He stormed out of the room, _____ the door behind him.

6 Shining his torch through the chain link fence, Todd was greeted by an angry _____ dog.

7 The figure _____ the window and reached inside.

8 The fan was _____ in the corner of the room.

4.2 Intensifiers

Choose the correct options (a, b or c) to complete the sentences.

1   The risks of this kind of technology are ___ greater than any potential benefit.

   a   intensely

   b   utterly

   c   considerably

2   All of the medical professionals that we spoke to said that the idea robots could perform complex surgery was ___ ridiculous.

   a   disastrously

   b   extremely

   c   utterly

3   To be honest, the results were ___ unexpected. I thought we'd need to run several more tests.

   a   considerably

   b   totally

   c   painfully

4   Seeing a computer program that I designed beat a human competitor is ___ satisfying.

   a   intensely

   b   totally

   c   disastrously

5   If we don't put the proper safety measures in place, the results could be ___ bad.

   a   disastrously

   b   utterly

   c   intensely

6   I am ___ sorry to announce that Maria Sanchez will be retiring from the field of robotics.

   a   utterly

   b   totally

   c   extremely

➤ Go back to page 45.

5.2 Prefixes

Choose the correct prefix to complete the sentences.

1   Levels of pollution were so high they needed to *decontaminate* / *uncontaminate* the river.

2   They were *disqualified* / *unqualified* from the race for cheating.

3   In order to improve travel times, they decided to *upgrade* / *downgrade* the metro system.

4   The solution was *unpossible* / *impossible* to put into place.

5   The company *misled* / *disled* the community about the development.

6   People don't use the train because they feel it is *overpriced* / *underpriced*.

7   The cost of building new road networks was significantly *underestimated* / *overestimated*.

8   The excellent infrastructure has allowed the city to *overperform* / *outperform* many similarly sized cities.

➤ Go back to page 55.

Communication Hub

3.1 Groups

A PREPARE Work in pairs. Use the pictures (a–g) to tell a story.

B PLAN Join another pair. Together work out the details of your story. Use narrative tenses to help describe the sequence of events.

➤ Go back to page 27.

1.2 Student A

Read the text and make notes about:

- who the person is and why they're famous
- any challenges they faced and how they overcame them
- any other interesting/relevant information

Emily Blunt

Emily Blunt was born in London in 1983. As a young girl, she felt confident and had a lot to say but unfortunately, she struggled because of a stutter. The stutter made it very difficult for Emily to say anything and between the ages of 12 and 13, she was badly bullied by other children. Strangely, whenever she spoke in a different accent or a funny voice, she lost the stutter and was able to communicate. Spotting her talent for different voices and for making people laugh, one of her teachers encouraged her to take part in the school play. But how could someone who struggled to speak stand up in front of the whole school and perform? Emily did the play in one of her funny voices and caught the acting bug. She has since gone on to win a BAFTA and a Golden Globe for her acting and has starred in many successful films such as *Sicario*, *The Girl on the Train* and *A Quiet Place*.

Glossary

stutter (n) to have difficulty saying something because you can't stop yourself from repeating the first sound of some words several times

➤ Go back to page 7.

5.2 Groups

A PLAN You're going to select three candidates to join the Mars One mission. Read the profiles and make notes on who you would like to select and why.

ADRIAN JENKINS

Leadership Has led teams of dozens of men in dangerous situations.
Personality traits Very determined and strong-minded. Always believes he is right. Not willing to listen to others.
Qualifications An MBA.
Unique skills Worked as paramedic. Is an expert in emergency situations.

LINA WANG

Leadership No leadership experience.
Personality traits Quickly forms strong relationships with others. A very creative problem-solver.
Qualifications Currently completing a PhD in Physics.
Unique Skills Is recognised as one of the most talented scientists in the world for her age. Three products she has designed have won international awards.

ANA RAMOS

Leadership Has led small teams of marine biologists.
Personality traits Excellent attention to detail. Very organised and well prepared.
Qualifications A PhD in Marine Biology.
Unique Skills Experience at spending time in small spaces. Has been on many long research trips to isolated places.

NICOS ALEXOPOULOS

Leadership Has led teams of surgeons for over ten years.
Personality traits Hard-working, with a never-give-up attitude. A perfectionist.
Qualifications Qualified doctor.
Unique Skills Has worked in many hospitals including many years with Doctors Without Borders in very difficult environments.

VIKTOR POPOV

Leadership No leadership experience.
Personality traits Prefers to spend time on his own. Finds relationships with others difficult.
Qualifications Engineering degree.
Unique Skills An experienced explorer. Has done survival training in the jungle and the desert.

GRACE ADEBAYO

Leadership Leads team of volunteers to help build schools and medical facilities in rural areas.
Personality traits Kind, caring and open-minded.
Qualifications A degree in Agriculture.
Unique Skills Experienced at growing food in difficult climates.

B DISCUSS Work in groups. Compare your choices in Exercise A. Agree on two candidates to join the Mars One mission.

➤ Go back to page 57.

Communication Hub

5.1 Pairs

A Work in pairs. Read the scenario and predict the cause and effect relationships between the pictures (1–10).

A chemical was sprayed to kill the mosquitoes.

In the early 1950s, an outbreak of malaria threatened the survival of the Dayak people of Borneo. Not knowing how to control the spread of the disease, the islanders turned to the outside world for help.

1 — Malaria spread throughout Borneo.
2
3
4
5
6
7
8
9
10 — Balance was restored.

B Work with another pair. Compare you ideas from Exercise A.

➤ Go back to page 51.

1.2 Student B

Read the text and write notes about:

- who the person is and why they're famous
- any challenges they faced and how they overcame them
- any other interesting/relevant information

Jean-Dominique Bauby

Jean-Dominique Bauby was born in France in 1952. He was an actor and author. He also edited the famous fashion magazine *Elle*. In December 1995, aged just 43, he suffered a massive stroke. When he finally woke up, he discovered he had been asleep for 20 days. Most of his body had been paralysed by the stroke and he had lost his speech. Despite his physical problems, he started writing the book *The Diving Bell and the Butterfly*. He did this by blinking his left eye while someone was reading the alphabet very slowly. He wrote and edited the book completely in his head while dictating one letter at a time. Unfortunately, two days after the book was published, he died. The book went on to be made into a film, which was nominated for four Oscars and won two Golden Globe Awards.

Glossary

stroke (n) a sudden change in the blood supply to the brain

➤ Go back to page 7.

W — structuring formal letters

A Read the letter and answer the questions.

1 What is the purpose of the letter?

2 Who will read it?

3 Why does the writer use a formal register?

B Match the parts of the letter (1–5) with their function (a–e).

a expected response

b reason for writing

c sign-off

d salutation or greeting

e information required

To: French language club
From: John

¹Dear Sir / Madam,

²I am writing to enquire about the French language club you organise to find out whether the club is suitable for me or not.

³Firstly, I was wondering if you could tell me how many members there are. Also, could you tell me when you meet and how often? I want to make sure it's possible for me to attend regularly. Could you also tell me how much it costs? Is there a joining fee and then a weekly fee to pay? Lastly, would it be possible to tell me the approximate level of the group members and whether we have any formal lessons as well?

⁴I would be grateful if you could let me know by email before the next meeting. Hopefully, I will be able to join before then. Thanks in advance for your help.

⁵Kind regards

John

C Complete the box with sentences from the letter.

Structuring formal letters
Saying why you're writing
I am writing to apply for …
1
Organising information
Could you let me know …?
2
Asking for a response
If you could …
3
Sign-off
Yours faithfully …
4

WRITING

A PREPARE Read the task below and make notes about who you are writing to, what you need to know and what action you expect them to take.

> You are keen to join the hiking club in your area. Write a letter of enquiry and find out:
> - how many members there are in the club
> - how often they organise walks and where they go
> - ask whether there are any fees involved in joining
> - what specialist equipment you need.

B PLAN Organise your notes into an appropriate structure for a letter of enquiry.

C WRITE Write your letter of enquiry. Use your plan to help you.

D EDIT Work in pairs. Edit your partner's essay. Check:
- spelling and punctuation
- all information in the task has been covered
- an appropriate structure/tone has been used

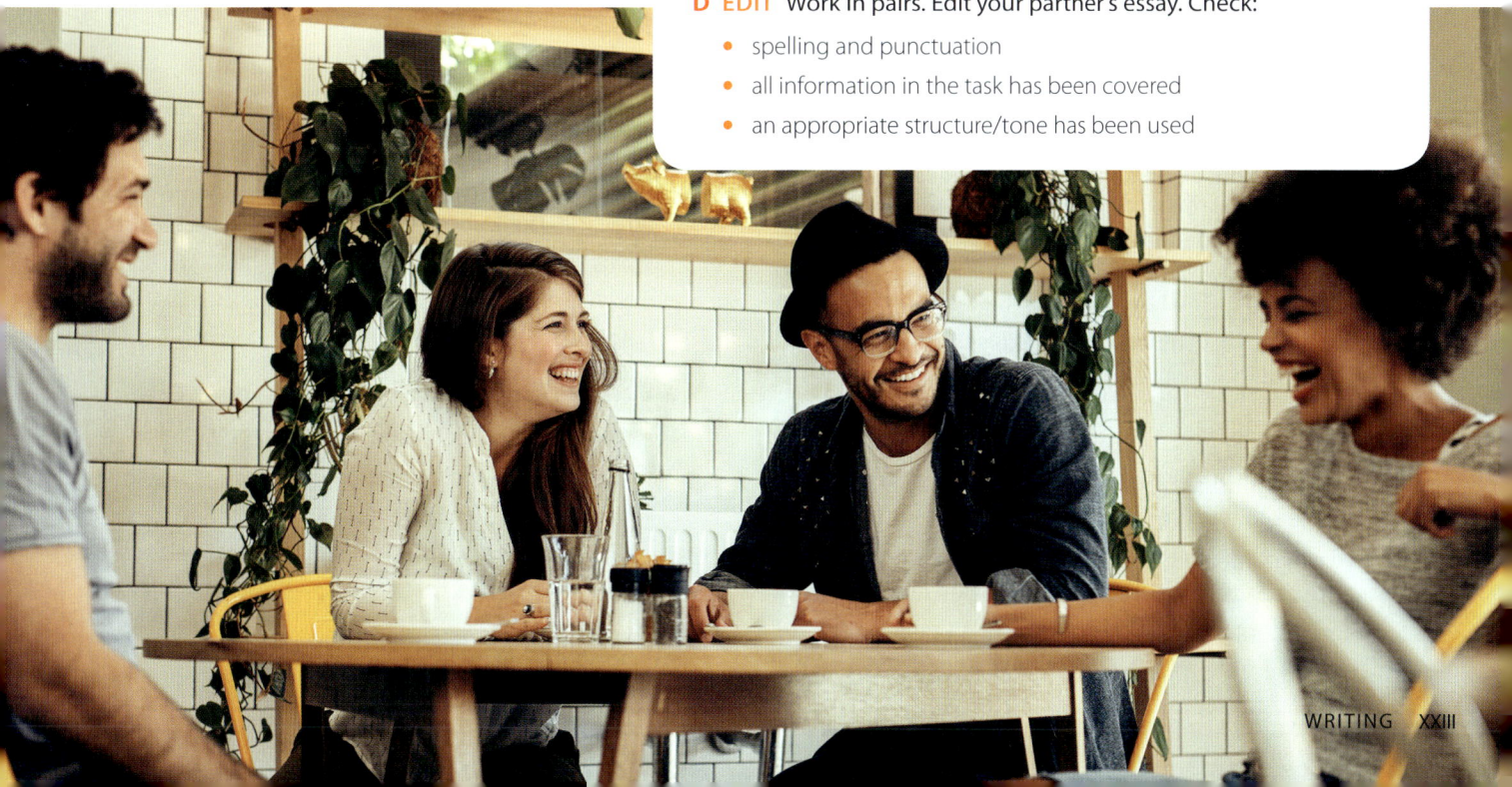

W — Using different structures to give advice

A Work in pairs. You are going to read an article titled *Clear the mess and clear your mind*. What advice do you think the author might give?

B Read the article quickly. Which of your ideas from Exercise A does the author mention?

Clear the mess and clear your mind

What better way to start the new year than getting rid of some clutter? Doing so will not only make your house feel more organised, but could also lower your stress levels. Hopefully, the following tips should help you get started!

Throw things away

We keep far more things than we really need to and many of these can be thrown away or given to someone else to use.

- Do you really need or like all of your clothes? Why not go through your wardrobe and see if there's anything you can donate to charity?
- If you don't watch it, listen to it or read it, sell it on eBay. You'll make a little bit of money and have more space!
- Don't forget to look in the garage. Most people use these areas to store things they just don't need or want.
- Don't keep broken things that you know you'll never fix.

Stay motivated

Decluttering can be hugely satisfying, but only if you can stay motivated. Use these basic rules to help you:

- Make sure you don't spend too long decluttering. If you are tired, take a break. It's much harder to make good decisions when you can't think properly!
- Don't leave a task incomplete. If you don't finish what you started, you're likely to become demotivated.

Good habits

Clutter can quickly build up again, so it's important to develop good habits for the future. Use these basic rules to help you:

- Avoid putting things into a pile. Putting them back where they belong will help keep things tidy.
- Remember to never buy something on impulse. You can always buy it later if you really want it.

C Read the article again. Complete the table with examples from the text.

Using different structures to give advice
if + present simple + imperative
1 _____
2 _____
negative imperative
3 _____
4 _____
5 _____
positive imperative
6 _____
7 _____

D Rewrite the sentences using the words in bold.

1 Drinking coffee after 9 pm is not a good idea.
   Avoid _____ .

2 Why not try putting $20 into a savings account every week?
   Try to _____ .

3 If you don't use your gym membership, cancel it.
   It's a good idea to _____ .

4 Perhaps you could turn your phone off in the evenings.
   Try _____ .

5 Try to do some exercise at least three times a week.
   Don't forget to _____ .

6 Recording the food you eat every day is a good idea.
   Remember to _____ .

WRITING

A PREPARE Work in pairs. Brainstorm advice you could give about one of these topics:

- reducing stress
- improving your diet
- getting fit

B PLAN Organise your notes from Exercise A into a plan for an article. Think about the clearest way to present your ideas, using headings where appropriate.

C WRITE Write your advice article. Use your plan to help you.

D EDIT Work in pairs. Edit your partner's essay. Check:

- spelling and punctuation
- use of expressions to give advice
- appropriacy of the ideas (e.g. Is the advice clear? Is it good advice?)

W— using adverbs to add detail to a story

A Work in pairs. What is the worst holiday experience you have ever had?

B Read the story and answer the questions. Underline the parts of the text that gives you the answers.

1 What did they regret?

2 Did anyone fall into the sea?

3 Where did they have to sleep?

Holiday from HELL

Two years ago, my wife and I took a summer holiday in Sicily, Italy. The town we were staying in was beautiful, but there wasn't a lot to do. So, a few days into our stay, we decided to book a boat trip to the volcanic Aeolian islands. I'd just bought a new camera, so I was really looking forward to trying it out in such an amazing place. However, the night before we were due to leave, a terrible storm hit the south coast of Italy, so we assumed our trip would be cancelled. The next morning, as we were strolling down to the harbour, the sea looked incredibly rough as the waves smashed against the rocks. Surprisingly, the trip went ahead anyway. We boarded the boat and waited nervously for it to leave. The waves were getting pretty violent and I thought about getting off several times but decided to wait and see if things would be better at sea. It was a decision that I was soon to regret as the boat rumbled out of the harbour.

At first, everything was strangely calm, and we wondered why we had been so nervous in the first place. But then the wind started to howl all around us. We rocked backwards and forwards as huge waves slammed violently against the boat, soaking us to the skin. Terrifyingly, benches were thrown from one side of the boat to the other and people all around us were sliding across the deck. Fortunately, no one fell over the side.

Finally, we reached the islands. We rapidly left the boat and sat shaking on the harbour wall. The staff assured us that the boat would return in three hours, but we were too terrified to go through that again. Strolling around the island, we tried desperately to find a hotel for the night so that we could return the next morning on the larger and safer car ferry. However, it was the peak of summer and all of the hotels were booked up so we had no choice but to spend the night on the beach. An exciting day out had swiftly turned into the trip from hell!

C Read the story again and put the events in the order they happened.

___ arranged a boat trip

___ nervously boarded the boat

___ searched desperately for a hotel

___ a terrible storm erupted

___ waves smashed across the boat

___ slept on the sandy beach

___ walked to the harbour expecting the trip to be cancelled

___ benches were thrown side to side and people slid across the deck

D SCAN Complete the box with the highlighted adverbs in the text.

Using adverbs to give detail to a story
We use adverbs of manner (e.g. *slowly*, _____, _____, _____) to talk about how something happens.
We use adverbs of stance (e.g. *strangely*, _____, _____, _____, _____,) to describe how we feel about something.

E Rewrite the sentences using the adverbs in bold.

1 It was incredible how dangerous the roads were on the island.
   incredibly
   The roads _____.

2 We were nervous as we waited for the rescue team to come.
   nervously
   We waited _____.

3 I was surprised the rescue team took such a long time to arrive.
   surprisingly
   The rescue team _____.

4 It didn't take long for the fire to spread through the building.
   rapidly
   The fire _____.

WRITING

A PREPARE You are going to write a short story about a nightmare journey or holiday. Make notes about:

- the location
- the people involved
- how you felt
- the key events
- contextual details (e.g. the weather, landscape, etc)

B PLAN Organise your notes from Exercise A into a plan for a short story.

C WRITE Write your short story. Use your plan to help you.

D EDIT Work in pairs. Edit your partner's story. Check:

- spelling and punctuation
- use of adverbs
- use of narrative tenses

W— structuring a for and against blog post

A Read the introduction to the blog post. What issue is the writer going to discuss?

B Work in pairs. Brainstorm ideas for and against the issue.

C Scan the blog post. Which of your ideas from Exercise B are mentioned?

About Blog Contact   Search

In order to deal with congestion in cities, some people think that private vehicles should be banned from city centres. Others, however, feel that this is an unrealistic solution and that alternatives would work more effectively. This post will consider both perspectives.

¹One of the arguments in favour of banning cars is that they are simply unnecessary if public transport is effective. The needs of individuals can arguably be met by heavy investment in public transportation and the replacement of roads with cycle paths. A good example of a city that has taken this idea to heart is Oslo, which aims to ban all cars from the city centre by 2019 – approximately six years before a nationwide city ban comes into effect. Oslo is planning to replace nearly 50 kilometres of road with cycle lanes by the time the city goes car-free.

²On the one hand, banning cars seems like a simple way to address congestion in city centres. Yet, on the other hand, serious investment is required to make this feasible. One issue is that extensive public transport networks would be required to replace cars in city centres. Many networks are seriously outdated or limited in their coverage. Furthermore, many countries simply do not have the financial means to build and extend their networks on such a scale.

³I believe that banning cars from city centres is only feasible in cities that already have an effective public transport system. For everywhere else, cars are simply the most efficient way to get around.

⁴To conclude, while many cities are making steps towards banning cars from city centres, doing so requires heavy investment which many countries may not be able to afford. Realistically, we are a long way from car-free city centres.

D Match the paragraphs (1–4) to their functions (a–d).

a Arguments for ___   **c** Conclusion ___

b Personal opinion ___   **d** Arguments against ___

E Complete the box with phrases from the blog.

Structuring a for and against blog post

Introduction
Many people think that …
1 _____

To give arguments for and against
Some people argue that …
Others think …
2 _____
3 _____
4 _____

To give examples / more information
For example …
5 _____

To give your opinion
I am convinced that …
6 _____

Conclusion
In conclusion, …
7 _____

WRITING

A PREPARE Read the blog topic and make notes of arguments for and against.

> **Building more cycle lanes is the best way to address pollution in city centres.**

B PLAN Organise your notes from Exercise A into a plan for a for and against blog post.

C WRITE Write your blog post. Use your notes to help you.

D EDIT Work in pairs. Edit your partner's blog. Check:
- spelling and punctuation
- use of phrases to structure their argument
- strength of ideas

W— describing problems and solutions

A Read the introduction to the problem/solution article. What is the main focus of the article?

> **Overcrowding in cities is among the principal dangers facing society today. This article will first look at some of the problems this causes and then suggest a number of possible solutions.**

B Work in pairs. Brainstorm possible problems and solutions for this topic.

C Scan the blog post. Which of your ideas from Exercise B are mentioned?

The main issue facing cities today is overcrowding, and the result is added pressure on public facilities. Schools, hospitals and roads are pushed to breaking point as the city struggles to keep up with the rapid population increase. A good example of this is the pressure placed on hospitals and doctors, who are expected to deal with growing numbers of patients despite no increase in staff. One way to tackle the increased pressure on public facilities is to regulate building. When building new housing, rules should be put in place to ensure that enough new facilities are constructed at the same time. For instance, for every 1000 new flats, a primary school and a doctor's surgery should be built by the construction firm.

One of the other foremost problems that occurs as a consequence of overcrowding is the increased levels of traffic. As a result, air pollution increases and traffic slows down. For example, in Mexico City, traffic has slowed to an average of around 10 kmph. One solution might be to build more cycle lanes around city centres. This will allow commuters to navigate the city more quickly and will lower the CO_2 emissions. One example where this has been done successfully is Copenhagen in Denmark, where hundreds of metres of cycle paths have been built.

In order to tackle the problems of overcrowding, cities should focus not only on building more housing but also on providing the infrastructure needed to support the growing population.

D Read the first paragraph again. Put the following in order to show the paragraph structure.

___ state the solution

_1_ state the problem

___ explain how this will solve the problem

___ show the results of the problem

___ give an example of the solution

___ give an example of the problem

E Complete the skills box with phrases from the article.

> ### Describing problems and solutions
>
> **Introduction**
> *X is one of the biggest issues we face …*
> 1 _____
>
> **Problems and results**
> *The biggest threat to …*
> *The foremost problem …*
> 2 _____
> 3 _____
>
> **Examples and results**
> *The result is …*
> 4 _____
> *A good example of this is …*
>
> **Solutions and explanations**
> *One way to tackle the issue of X is to …*
> 5 _____
> *This will allow …*

WRITING

A **PREPARE** Work in pairs. Brainstorm problems and solutions in response to the following:

> **What are some of the difficulties of living and working in a megacity?**

B **PLAN** Organise your ideas from Exercise A into a plan for an article.

C **WRITE** Write your article. Use your plan to help you.

D **EDIT** Work in pairs. Edit your partner's article. Check:

- spelling and punctuation
- structure and organisation
- strength of ideas

Irregular Verbs

Infinitive	Past simple	Past participle
be	was/were	been
become	became	become
begin	began	begun
break	broke	broken
bring	brought	brought
build	built	built
buy	bought	bought
can	could	(been able to)
catch	caught	caught
choose	chose	chosen
come	came	come
cost	cost	cost
cut	cut	cut
drink	drank	drunk
eat	ate	eaten
fall	fell	fallen
feel	felt	felt
find	found	found
forget	forgot	forgotten
get	got	got
give	gave	given
go	went	gone/been
grow	grew	grown
have	had	had
hear	heard	heard
hit	hit	hit
hold	held	held
hurt	hurt	hurt
keep	kept	kept
know	knew	known
leave	left	left
lend	lent	lent
let	let	let

Infinitive	Past simple	Past participle
lose	lost	lost
make	made	made
mean	meant	meant
meet	met	met
must	had to	had to
pay	paid	paid
put	put	put
read	read	read
ride	rode	ridden
run	ran	run
say	said	said
see	saw	seen
sell	sold	sold
send	sent	sent
set	set	set
shut	shut	shut
sing	sang	sung
sit	sat	sat
sleep	slept	slept
speak	spoke	spoken
spell	spelt/spelled	spelt/spelled
spend	spent	spent
stand	stood	stood
steal	stole	stolen
take	took	taken
teach	taught	taught
tell	told	told
think	thought	thought
throw	threw	thrown
understand	understood	understood
wear	wore	worn
win	won	won
write	wrote	written

PHONETIC SYMBOLS

Single vowels

/ɪ/	fish	/fɪʃ/
/iː/	bean	/biːn/
/ʊ/	foot	/fʊt/
/uː/	shoe	/ʃuː/
/e/	egg	/eg/
/ə/	mother	/ˈmʌðə/
/ɜː/	word	/wɜːd/
/ɔː/	talk	/tɔːk/
/æ/	back	/bæk/
/ʌ/	bus	/bʌs/
/ɑː/	arm	/ɑːm/
/ɒ/	top	/tɒp/

Diphthongs

/ɪə/	ear	/ɪə/
/eɪ/	face	/feɪs/
/ʊə/	tourist	/ˈtʊərɪst/
/ɔɪ/	boy	/bɔɪ/
/əʊ/	nose	/nəʊz/
/eə/	hair	/heə/
/aɪ/	eye	/aɪ/
/aʊ/	mouth	/maʊθ/

Consonants

/p/	pen	/pen/	/s/	snake	/sneɪk/
/b/	bag	/bæg/	/z/	zoo	/zuː/
/t/	tea	/tiː/	/ʃ/	shop	/ʃɒp/
/d/	dog	/dɒg/	/ʒ/	television	/ˈtelɪvɪʒən/
/tʃ/	chip	/tʃɪp/	/m/	map	/mæp/
/dʒ/	jazz	/dʒæz/	/n/	name	/neɪm/
/k/	cake	/keɪk/	/ŋ/	ring	/rɪŋ/
/g/	girl	/gɜːl/	/h/	house	/haʊs/
/f/	film	/fɪlm/	/l/	leg	/leg/
/v/	verb	/vɜːb/	/r/	road	/rəʊd/
/θ/	thing	/θɪŋ/	/w/	want	/wɒnt/
/ð/	these	/ðiːz/	/j/	yes	/jes/

Audioscripts

UNIT 1

Lesson 1.1 Listening, Exercise B

1.1 M = Mark   S = Sarah   F = Fyodor   A = Alana
M = Martin   Y = Yumi

Conversation 1

M: Hello. I haven't seen you here before.

S: Er, no, I've just joined actually. This is my first Get Together.

M: Oh, well, you chose a good group. Everyone here's pretty friendly and we all have a similar level of ability, which helps.

S: That's a relief. I've been learning for about a year or so now. How about you? Have you been playing long?

M: Er, yeah a little bit longer … for about two and a half years. I think I'm alright but I'm no expert.

S: Yeah, me neither. Do you ever perform at all?

M: Me? Ha ha! No, no. I'm definitely not good enough for that. I'm just doing this for fun really. How about you?

S: Yeah, same really. It just seemed like a fun thing to do. Anyway, who's leading the group tonight?

M: Er, Lucy, I think. She's actually a professional musician, so we're in good hands.

S: Well I certainly need all the help I can get!

Conversation 2

F: Excuse me, could you tell me where the changing rooms are?

A: Sure. I'm going there now if you want to come with me. I'm Alana by the way. You're new to the Get Together, aren't you?

F: Er, yeah I am. I've just moved to the area. I was a member of the running Get Together before I moved here.

A: Where were you living before?

F: I was living in Birmingham but I got a new job, so I moved to London. I'm living in Clapham at the moment, but I might actually move.

A: Oh, really? How come?

F: Well I like Clapham but my flat is a really long way from the station and I don't really get on with my flatmates.

A: Oh, fair enough. Why don't you like them?

F: Well, one of them works night shifts so he always comes home really late and the other just spends all his time in his room. Maybe I should just look for a place on my own.

A: Maybe, although flat shares can be pretty fun if you can find the right people.

F: I suppose so. Who do you live with?

A: A couple of friends I've known since university. They can definitely be annoying sometimes, but I wouldn't want to live with anyone else.

F: Sounds fun. Anyway, have you been running long?

A: Er, no, not long really. I just wanted to, you know, get more into sports and I loved running at college, so I thought I'd give it a go.

F: Fair enough. Are you planning to enter any races this summer or is it a bit too soon?

A: Well, I was actually thinking of signing up for the 10K at the end of September.

F: The one in Richmond? You definitely should. Ten kilometres sounds like a long way, but it's actually not too bad. I just put in a lot of training and was completely fine on the day.

A: OK, good to know. Maybe we could do it together?

F: Ha ha! Maybe. I'm doing a half marathon the week before though, so I might not have the energy for another race!

Conversation 3

M: Excuse me, could you tell me where I sign in for the book club Get Together?

Y: Er, yeah, right here actually. I'm running the group tonight. Can I take your name, please?

M: It's Martin Pajak.

Y: Oh, yes. I remember your name from your emails. Could I ask you to fill out this form when you get a chance? No rush to return it. Have you had time to finish the book yet?

M: Er, just about! I really like Haruki Murakami.

Y: Oh, really? Me too. Which is your favourite Murakami novel?

M: Um, probably *Norwegian Wood*, but I also loved *After Dark*.

Y: *Norwegian Wood* was the first Murakami book that I ever read. I thought it was amazing.

M: Oh, well if you like Murakami, you'd probably like Banana Yoshimoto. Especially her first novel, *Kitchen*.

Lesson 1.2 Listening, Exercise B

1.5 P = Presenter   R = Richard

P: Now we all know that friends are important, but according to our next guest, the type of friends we choose can have a dramatic impact on how successful we are. Here to explain why, is the psychologist Richard Bonnel. Richard, welcome to the show.

R: Thanks for having me.

P: So Richard, we all have hundreds of friends nowadays …

R: Well, we all know hundreds of people on Facebook, Twitter and other social media sites but how many are actually our friends is debatable. Realistically, research tells us that we can't maintain a friendship group of more than 50 people and, you know, in fact it's probably much smaller if we consider just the people we regularly communicate with.

P: So what type of friends are important to have in your life?

R: Well, our research shows that very successful people surround themselves with six different types of friend. Not six friends but six types. We all need a loyal best friend. Someone who will support us no matter what happens. Someone who knows everything about you. They know all of your secrets but they still love you anyway.

P: I definitely have one of those. There's no way I'd ever let them on this show. They have far too many stories about me!

R: You probably don't need to worry. You can trust them to keep any embarrassing secrets private! Well, they might let one or two things out just for fun … The next type is really important to make your life more interesting. This person is an open-minded adventurer. They always force us into new and different situations. They challenge us. They push us to try new things. They are easy-going and open to new ideas, cultures and activities. None of these things stress them out. Basically, they break us out of our normal routine.

P: I actually think I'm that friend to a lot of people. I'm always taking people to new places and making them do new things.

R: I don't doubt it. These people, they're usually great with people, self-confident and like the attention of others.

P: Are you saying I'm arrogant?

R: No, these people aren't arrogant. They just have a lot of self-belief. Other people probably love it as they are much more cautious than you. You add a bit of spice to their life! Another type of friend that people need, is one they probably don't always like or want. That's someone who is really honest even when it upsets you.

P: How is that useful?

R: Well, this person will tell you when your hair looks awful or your clothes look terrible. They'll tell you when you're being self-centred and should think about others more. Or they'll tell you you are being stubborn and need to be more flexible. It's tough to hear, but it's usually true.

P: I do have a friend like that. She's very down-to-earth. She just does everything in this very sensible, practical way. I guess she is a helpful person to have around!

R: Right, exactly. Equally, it's important to not just surround ourselves with like-minded people. We should have some friends who are the complete opposite to us.

P: Why would you want to do that? Surely you'd just argue?

R: Perhaps, but it opens your mind to different ways of seeing the world. It makes you a more accepting person.

P: True. So, are there any other types of people we should surround ourselves with?

R: Well, the last two are not really types of people but friends we should try to make because of our circumstances. We all move around much more nowadays and often have no idea who our neighbours are, but they are important to know. Dependable neighbours can help in difficult situations and make you feel happier about where you live.

P: Oh, that is so true. I'm really happy where I live now and it's mainly because of the people living near me.

R: How about work? Are you happy at work?

P: Well, I think I'm pretty lucky. I actually love my job.

R: It's vital that you do. Successful people always work with people they like. Most people spend at least 50% of their waking hours at work. On top of that, people commute to work, work overtime, think about work. It can take over your life. Imagine feeling isolated at work. No one to chat to. Having no witty people to have a laugh with would make work very boring. A depressing thought, isn't it?

P: Now you put it like that, I think I might need to find a new job!

UNIT 2

Lesson 2.1 Listening, Exercise C
2.1 P = Presenter

P: OK, let's move onto our next topic. Now, according to a recent survey conducted by The Institute for Social Research, the British public are terrible at sticking to their New Year's resolutions. Apparently, 43% of people surveyed broke their resolution within the first month and 86% lasted less than a year.

To test the accuracy of these results, we sent reporter Emily Hussan out onto the streets of London to see just how many of you have managed to successfully give something up for the New Year.

Lesson 2.1 Listening, Exercise D
**2.2 P = Presenter   S1 = Speaker 1   S2 = Speaker 2
S3 = Speaker 3   S4 = Speaker 4   S5 = Speaker 5**

Speaker 1

P: Sorry, excuse me. We're interviewing people about whether they've managed to stick to their New Year's Resolutions. Did you make any this year?

S1: Yeah, I did actually. Well, the whole family did really. My family and I felt that, well, we really didn't spend enough time together. You know, I found we hardly ever spoke to each other. We, er, just sat around using our various devices in our own little worlds. We've been living without smartphones and tablets for a couple of months now. I bought everyone really old-fashioned phones that you could only call and text on.

P: How did your children feel about that?

S1: Oh, well, the children went crazy! They were really mad at us!

P: Was it worth it?

S1: Definitely! It was really hard to cope with at first, but since then our lives have, well, changed for the better. We've been spending more time together as a family. And, um, I think we have a better relationship. And you know what? We are all sleeping better as a result of giving up technology.

Speaker 2

P: So, did you try to give anything up for the New Year?

S2: Yeah, I've actually given up coffee.

P: Oh, really? Why?

S2: Well, at the end of last year, I was really stressed at work and it had started to affect my sleep. I was only getting about two or three hours every night and this put me in a bad mood the next day. I thought about doing more exercise, but I've never really been a gym kind of person. Then I thought, 'Maybe I drink too much coffee'. I used to drink, like, four or five cups a day, but I cut this down to two, then stopped entirely to try and help me sleep better.

P: Well done! And did it work?

S2: Absolutely! I've been living without coffee for months now and get at least seven hours sleep every night. You should try it!

Speaker 3

P: Did you make any resolutions back in January?

S3: Well, I always knew that I didn't have a great diet but didn't realise just how bad sugar is for you. Obviously it can affect your weight, but it can also lead to heart disease, diabetes … even some forms of cancer. Anyway, I read this article that said you should only have a maximum of six teaspoons a day, and I was having way more than that.

P: What, like cakes and chocolate and stuff?

S3: Well yeah, but there's also lots of sugar in things you wouldn't expect like yoghurt, bread …

P: Bread?

S3: Yep! Most processed foods have added sugar. Anyway, I've managed to lose a bit of weight since cutting down and it's really made me think about my diet in general. I've only had three chocolate bars this month!

Speaker 4

P: So have you made any changes since the New Year?

S4: Not through choice! My car's in the garage at the moment, so I've been cycling to work for the past two weeks.

P: No … sorry, I meant resolutions.

S4: Oh, I see. Yes, well this is going to sound weird, but I've stopped using shampoo.

P: Um, really?

S4: Ha ha! Yep. I've only washed my hair twice this month. Pretty disgusting, huh?

P: It doesn't sound great to be honest.

S4: Well, my hair was pretty greasy at first and I'm sure I didn't smell too great either, but after a few weeks my body seemed to adjust.

P: So why did you decide to give it up? To help the environment?

S4: Er, no. A lot of people say shampoo contains harmful chemicals, but I don't really think that's true. I actually gave it up because of a friend. She said that my hair was in really bad condition and suggested I try washing it less. I haven't used shampoo since December and my hair feels great. And I've saved loads of money!

Speaker 5

P: Did you try to give anything up for New Year?

S5: Er, no not really. I haven't given anything up for ages.

P: When did you last give something up?

S5: Um, I'm not sure really. Well actually, I've been vegan for five years now. I wanted to reduce my carbon footprint, which I've managed to do.

P: Oh, really? How's that possible?

S5: Well, it takes so much more water to produce meat.

P: Really? Why?

S5: Well, obviously the animals we eat need to drink water and a surprisingly large amount of water is used to grow their food.

P: Oh, right. How do you feel personally?

S5: I feel healthier. I've lost weight and have more energy.

Lesson 2.2 Listening, Exercise B
2.5 I = Interviewer   F = Frank   K = Katie

I: Many of us have dreamed of escaping the rat race and getting away from our stressful lives, but few of us have ever actually taken the plunge. Well, on today's show we have one family who have done just that. Joining us from their beach-front home is Frank Gerrard and his daughter Katie. Thanks for joining us today. It looks beautiful there! Can you hear me OK?

F: Yes, I can hear you.

I: Now, you've made quite a dramatic change to your life. What were you doing before?

F: I had a terrible job! I used to work long hours and it was stressful. I was exhausted and overworked. I used to dream of living a quieter and more peaceful life … You know, getting back to nature and that sort of thing. So, I quit my job, sold the family home and we moved here.

I: Wow! That's quite a dramatic change! How's it all been going?

F: It's been amazing! We have a small plot of land next to our house and we grow a lot of our own food. I go fishing and hunting every day.

I: Is there a local shop?

F: There is, but we hardly ever go. I want to grow or catch everything.

I: So was the change easy for you?

F: Actually, it was a lot harder getting used to the new lifestyle than I thought it would be. When I worked in an office, I was so physically tired all the time because I just sat at my desk all day writing emails. I never really got up and walked around until it was time to go home, and even then I just walked to the station and sat on a train for half an hour. Now I have so many more physical tasks to do to produce the food we need. I'm used to getting up at six o'clock every day now and working hard until it gets dark. Financially, it has also been much harder but we're getting used to it.

I: Would you make the same decision again?

F: For me, definitely! I wouldn't change a thing. As for my family, well I'm not so sure. They miss London a lot and actually, I'm so busy all the time that we don't really spend that much more time together. We also have way less money now – not that there's much to spend it on!

I: Well this seems like a good point to bring in your daughter. Katie, how did you feel about the decision?

K: I understand why Dad did it. Back in London, he'd complain about his work constantly. He hated it. Mum just wanted him to be happier. But, well I think it was a stupid idea. He's just having a midlife crisis! Why would anyone want to move here?

I: So, you're not happy there then?

K: No. I used to see my friends all the time in London. We'd go shopping or hang out in the park. What is there to do here? Walk up another mountain? The internet is terrible as well. When I was bored in London, I used to watch Netflix on my phone or listen to something on Spotify. That kind of thing is just out of the question now because our internet connection is so bad. We also don't seem to have any money now, which is weird – shouldn't we be better off?

I: OK, and what's school like there?

K: It's the worst thing ever! I'm homeschooled now. There's a small school on the island, but my parents want me to take UK exams, so Mum is teaching us. I never ever leave the house!

I: Do you think you'll grow to love it?

K: No! I'm quite stressed actually. What job can I do here? Where will I go to university? I'm getting used to being isolated from everyone, but I need to think about my future. In London, I would always think about the exciting jobs and opportunities I could have in the future. I don't want a life like this – all day collecting food. It's boring!

I: Are there any positives about the move?

K: Seriously? No. Well, to be fair, I do enjoy swimming and sunbathing every day, but generally no, I'm bored a lot of the time. I guess I'm not used to it yet.

F: Well, our youngest loves it here. London isn't great for young children. I was always too worried to let him play outside alone. Now he's out there all day! He would hate to move back to London. It isn't great for teenagers though, so it might change as he gets older.

K: It definitely will. He's going to be so bored!

I: Well, thank you both for joining us.

UNIT 3

Lesson 3.1 Listening, Exercise C
3.1 I = Interviewer   P = Paul   H = Hayley   L = Lee

I: OK, welcome back to the show. Tonight we're talking about extreme sports. Why do so many people take part in such dangerous activities? Where's the fun in putting yourself at such risk? Maybe our next caller can help answer some of these burning questions. Paul, what dangerous sport do you do and why?

P: I'm into climbing. Especially free climbing.

I: When did you first get into climbing?

P: When I was four years old, my dad took me walking in the foothills of the Alps. I can still remember the snow crunching under our feet as we walked together. We always had a lot of fun, but I didn't really get into climbing until I was 17. I remember standing in front of a really steep rock face and thinking, 'Can I do this?'.

I: When did you move onto free climbing?

P: Probably about ten years later. By that point I'd become a pretty good climber and wanted a new challenge. I love the excitement, fear and challenge of it. My father thought it was a brilliant idea because he'd been a good climber as well, but my mother was terrified.

I: Have you ever had any accidents?

P: Well, I've had lots of terrifying moments. Once, I was high up the side of a mountain in Argentina, when the wind started to pick up. It was too dangerous to climb down, so I just had to hold on and wait. In some places, there are also these tiny wooden bridges attached to the side of the mountain to help you get from one ledge to another. Sometimes the wood groans under your weight, which can be a bit scary, but so far none have ever actually broken!

I: OK, so what's the most dangerous thing that's ever happened to you?

P: Well, a few years ago I was in South Africa with a few of my friends and we'd nearly finished the first part of an all-day climb. I was just pulling myself up when I saw a huge snake right in front of me. I am terrified of snakes, so I just froze as it started to hiss and arch backwards. I waited for another few minutes, not moving, and then it just seemed to get bored and slithered back into a crack in the rock. It was the most terrifying moment ever and it had nothing to do with climbing!

I: Thanks for calling in, Paul. Hope you don't meet any more snakes on your climbs.

I: We have our second caller, Hayley, with us now. Hayley, what dangerous sport are you into?

H: Potholing!

I: What, climbing through caves and things?

H: Yeah, that's right. It's great fun, actually.

I: Hmm …, not sure I'd enjoy it. Anyway, how long have you been potholing for?

H: I first got into potholing at university. There was a climbing and caving society that I joined. I had done a lot of climbing but I'd never done any potholing before. It was amazing!

I: How does it compare to climbing?

H: With climbing, you can see a lot of the route in front of you. Potholing is so dark, and the spaces can be really small, so it's difficult to plan your next move. Often, you start at the entrance to a cave and simply walk in, but within a few hundred metres you have crawled on your belly, swum underwater, and squeezed your body through tiny gaps. The challenges are just so much more varied.

I: And is it a dangerous sport?

H: It's more dangerous than it sounds. You can suffer from a lack of oxygen or too much carbon dioxide. You can get trapped. You can drown when there's a sudden storm. You can even fall to your death climbing. There are literally hundreds of ways you can die!

I: Sounds frightening! What was your most terrifying experience?

H: Once, I got lost when I was deep underground in Mexico. It can be silent for just a few minutes and all you can hear is water trickling around you. It's actually quite worrying because you have no maps and no way of communicating with people outside and getting help. Luckily, we managed to get back out the way we had come. By then we had been lost underground for several hours. It was terrifying and took me weeks to get over!

I: Thank you, Hayley. I have to say, potholing sounds terrifying! So now on to our last caller, Lee. Good evening, Lee.

L: Good evening!

I: So, Lee, what extreme sport are you into?

L: I'm a free runner.

I: OK, so when did you first get into it?

L: It started from when I was a child. I used to do gymnastics when I was young, so I was always into climbing and jumping. Then a friend at school showed me a video of a group of people free running and I thought, 'Why not give it a try?'

I: What do you enjoy most about free running?

L: Well, it makes you look at cities in different ways to other people. People often don't even look up when they walk around a city. They focus on everything at eye level – shops, people, cars. You actually really appreciate the architecture more from up high. Every city is a new physical challenge. I get excited and my adrenalin starts pumping!

I: How dangerous is free running?

L: It can be very dangerous. You need to be very aware of your own ability and try not to push yourself too hard. Unfortunately, because it is competitive, people are always pushing themselves to do more and more dangerous things. I have broken a lot of bones. Once, when I jumped between two buildings, I slipped and fell 20 metres. Luckily, I didn't break anything. This other time though, I fell just a couple of metres and I broke my ankle. I can still hear my ankle snap as I landed. It was so painful!

I: Oh, wow! That sounds horrible. Anyway, thanks for joining us, Lee. OK, listeners – we're just going to a short commercial break before we take our next caller.

Lesson 3.2 Listening, Exercise B
3.5 N = Narrator

Chapter 2 – Phobias and rational fears

Suddenly, you see something in the corner of your eye. Your palms start sweating, your heart beats faster and your muscles become tense. A tiny spider is crawling across the bathroom wall …

Why is it that many of us fear things that are, relatively speaking, completely harmless, yet don't think twice about real, everyday risks such as driving to work or heart disease?

The ability to calculate risk is essential to the survival of any species. Indeed, one of the most primitive human instincts is to assess our environment for potential threats. This heightened awareness of our surroundings is controlled by a section of the brain called the amygdala. It is responsible for our fear, anger, sadness, our levels of aggression. It determines how we should react to the things we see before us. Is that a tiger waiting in the bushes or just a trick of the light? Should we run away or stay and fight? This response – often referred to as 'fight or flight' – is what makes our heart beat faster and our palms start to sweat. This is actually an essential human instinct, but it's worth noting that for some, the response seems to be overly sensitive. They perceive threats where most people wouldn't and are generally far more anxious as a result. A bit like an overly sensitive car alarm that goes off every time somebody walks by.

So it is the amygdala that triggers our initial reaction to a perceived threat. But how do we determine whether the threat is real or not? For this, we rely on the hippocampus and the prefrontal cortex. They compare contextual information with our memories and experience, and decide whether we should be afraid or not. This is useful, as it allows us to decide, for example, to run away when we see a snake in the jungle but remain calm when we see one in a zoo. Essentially, the decision-making part of our brain can tell the emotional part to relax when there is no real threat.

The fact that we rely on our knowledge and experience to determine our emotional response is key to understanding our fears. If, for example, you had a terrifying experience with a dog when you were younger, this is highly likely to influence your reaction to them now. Similarly, if your only knowledge of an airline company is that one of their planes crashed recently, you might well be too afraid to fly with them, even if their overall safety record is very good. Although we are capable of remembering facts or statistics, humans tend to focus on the emotional and the dramatic. For example, according to Cancer Research UK, skin cancer leads to around two and half thousand deaths every year. Statistically, this is definitely something worth worrying about. In comparison, there are very few plane crashes every year. Yet when we go on holiday, many of us worry more about the plane crashing than whether or not we remembered to pack our sun cream.

Whilst our brains are constructed to help us identify, assess and react to potential threats, the heighted levels of anxiety this may cause can actually have a hugely negative effect on our bodies. For example, high levels of stress have a negative impact on the immune system, potentially leading to an increased risk of depression, heart disease and diabetes. And unfortunately, it seems that modern society is designed to increase stress and anxiety. We've become accustomed to 24-hour news coverage, instant access to information and a constant flow of messages, yet it could well be that instead of improving our lives, these all have a negative impact on our physical and mental health. If this is true, how we adapt to our increasingly connected world will be fundamental to our continued survival as a species.

UNIT 4

Lesson 4.1 Listening, Exercise C
4.1 P = Presenter   L = Lucy   H = Hadiyah   F = Frank

P: Aldbury is a small village in Hertfordshire, England. Like many other villages in this area, not a lot has changed here over the years, but for these three residents, life is about to change forever.

Lucy Warner has just graduated from Tring Secondary School and is going to start a law degree at Oxford in the autumn of next year. However, as she's never left Aldbury, she wants to take a year out to go travelling. When I spoke to her, she was busy packing her bags.

L: Can you pass me that bag? The red one behind you …

P: Sure. First of all, congratulations on graduating!

L: Thanks!

P: So, when do you leave?

L: Next Sunday!

P: Wow! So soon.

L: I know! Scary!

P: So, anything specific planned?

L: Well, um, I'm flying to Paris as I have a friend there. Then I'm taking the train to Spain, where I'm staying for a couple of months.

P: Oh right. Why so long in Spain?

L: I want to improve my Spanish. I speak a bit, but it's well, just tourist Spanish really. I'm starting a month-long course in Spanish in September. The lessons are three days a week from nine to four.

P: That sounds great.

L: Yeah, I don't know. It's just a bit of fun really. I don't really need another language – everyone there speaks some English anyway!

P: Sounds cool though. Any other exciting plans?

L: I'm really excited about taking the Trans-Siberian Express across Russia into Asia. I think it'll be amazing, a once in a lifetime experience. After that I'll probably spend quite a bit of time in China. Then, I'm going to visit as many countries as I can.

P: All without flying?

L: Well I'm definitely flying to Australia! I want to work there for a few months and then I might go to the States. I don't know if I'll have enough money, though.

P: Another person from Aldbury about to have a massive life change is Hadiyah Khan. Hadiyah is expecting her first baby. When I spoke to her, she was busy decorating the nursery. So, big changes ahead for you.

H: Yeah, I'm a little worried about it all actually!

P: Yeah, I think that's only natural. When's the baby due?

H: At the end of May, although apparently first babies are always late! A lot of our time is going to be spent getting things ready for the baby.

P: Do you know if it's a boy or a girl?

H: We don't – we wanted to keep it a surprise. My husband thinks it's going to be a girl, though.

P: Oh really? Why?

H: Everyone in our family has had girls!

P: Have you chosen any names yet?

H: No, we can't decide. There's the possibility of naming her Farrah after my nan or Nabila after my husband's nan. If it's a boy, who knows?

P: So, how do you feel?

H: I'm so excited! I've always dreamt of having children. I can't wait for everyone to meet our new baby. I know it's going to be exhausting, though. My sister has two children and I can see it isn't easy. But, you know, it'll be a lot of fun as well. I'm honestly just really excited! One thing I am worried about though is getting everything done. Parents are always really busy, so I'm definitely going to have to get better at managing my time.

P: At another stage of their life is Frank Schmitt. Having worked in the local bank for the last 30 years, Frank is now finally retiring. When I caught up with Frank, he was busy buying fishing equipment.

F: What do you think of this fishing rod?

P: Um, I have no idea – I don't know much about fishing to be honest!

F: Me neither. It's just something I finally have time to do.

P: That's right, you're retiring soon.

F: I am, I am, and I can't wait!

P: Do you think you'll miss work?

F: I suppose there's the risk of getting bored, but I doubt it. Everyone wants to retire, don't they? I'll probably just spend the first few months at home relaxing but then we're planning a big holiday.

P: A cruise?

F: No, but another typical pensioner trip! We have bought a huge caravan and we're going to travel to different places in the States for a year.

P: Fantastic! Where are you going to go?

F: We haven't planned it exactly. I'm excited to see some of the famous landmarks – the Statue of Liberty, for example. I've been to New York several times, but I've never seen the Statue of Liberty! We're going to start in New York and head down to Florida. After that I'm not sure. I'm looking forward to being more spontaneous!

P: I loved Seattle. You should go there.

F: Really? That's a good idea. I'll add it to the list!

Lesson 4.2 Listening, Exercise B
P = Presenter   M = Mark   S = Sarah

4.5

P: Good morning, everyone. Welcome to today's debate. Transport is changing rapidly around the world. More and more cars are becoming electric. Drones are being used for deliveries. So, of all the future predictions around transport and travel, which are most likely to come true? To discuss this with me today are Sarah Atkinson, technology blogger and editor at *The Neo Futurist*, and Mark Edwards, transport correspondent for *The Evening Express*. So, first let's talk about driverless cars – do you think we will see these on our roads any time soon?

M: Definitely! The way we get around is going to be entirely transformed. It's not a matter of if, but when this happens. These are incredibly exciting times!

P: Sarah, what do you think?

S: Sorry, but that is absolutely ridiculous. I firmly believe there is no chance driverless cars will become popular. How can a car make a decision about what to do in a dangerous situation? Should it protect the driver at all costs? What if doing so might mean injuring somebody else? What does it do then? I just think it would be incredibly dangerous to have driverless cars on the road.

M: People's reactions and decision-making are absolutely terrible! It's undoubtedly true that driverless cars will have more consistent and quicker reactions than most drivers.

S: Perhaps, but it's still slightly concerning. Driverless cars often crash during testing. A driverless bus crashed in its first hour of tests in Las Vegas! It's a dangerous development and we simply don't need it.

M: But it would greatly improve our lives! We could work in the car on the way to work. We could have a second car that took the kids to school. You could jump in and out of driverless taxis just paying with your card.

S: The level of associated risk is crazy! Imagine the car taking your kids to school had an accident. It's a terrifying idea, but fortunately I think it's highly unlikely to happen any time soon.

P: OK, so what about the Hyperloop? Elon Musk's vision of future trains? A pod travels through a tunnel with no friction or air resistance, making it a very fast and efficient way of travelling.

M: Well, I for one think they're an incredibly safe alternative to our current train systems. They could also cut journey times down by 80 to 90%. Imagine that. A four-hour journey could be completed in less than an hour!

S: Yes, they are very safe, but it won't happen. A Hyperloop train has to be in a fixed tunnel using air pressure and magnets to move the train. The big problem is that they are likely to run just between a few points that are miles apart and just go past all of the other big places in between. They will literally go straight past millions of passengers. Governments simply won't spend the money and companies won't either because it will be hard to make a profit.

M: Nonsense! Hyperloop train systems are widely expected to happen. Countries all around the world are investing time and money into their own Hyperloop systems. They're undoubtedly cheaper than building a normal high-speed train and travel times will be greatly reduced. Dubai to Abu Dhabi, normally a two-hour drive, would take just 12 minutes on a Hyperloop train! Why wouldn't cities invest in it?

P: I can imagine some of these developments happening – especially things that save significant time, like the Hyperloop train, and things that free up personal time, like driverless cars. I can imagine companies investing in and developing these ideas because they could make a lot of money, but what about something more futuristic, like the flying cars we see in movies?

M: This always seems like something purely from science fiction, but I don't think flying cars are actually that unrealistic. The technology isn't that far off …

S: Oh, come on. I think you're exaggerating there! We're at least 25 years away from anything like a flying car.

M: Hmm, I don't think so. Dubai police already have self-driving cars and robot police officers. Now they're adding a flying bike to their force. It will greatly improve response times in cities with serious traffic problems.

S: The laws and the health and safety issues here would be frightening!

M: Yes, but society has dealt with major changes before. Imagine what it was like on the early passenger planes taking people on holiday.

That must have been surprising to society and lots of rules and laws must have been needed, but society coped and moved on.

P: Actually, that brings me to my next point. What about the travel industry? How do you see that changing?

M: Well, I think we're likely to see hypersonic jets and space tourism in the not too distant future.

S: Space tourism? I can't see that really taking off – if you'll excuse the pun! There may be a small market for it, but only amongst the super rich.

M: Well, we'll see about that. But when it comes to hypersonic jets, I've got no doubt that the technology is improving all the time and it's quite likely it will become significantly cheaper over time. That means it would be affordable for most people. The Sabre jet developed in the UK could get you from Britain to Australia in four hours. That's nearly 20 hours quicker!

S: You seem incredibly focused on speed! I'd be much more interested in a solar plane that was better for the environment. Even if it took me an extra day to get somewhere! In general people think more about the environment today. It's a bigger concern than speed.

M: That could happen as well. I absolutely love the idea of getting places quicker, though. Who wants to sit on a plane for two days? I somewhat agree with your opinion on space travel, though. It's an experience rather than a holiday.

P: Thank you both. Now let's move on to the Q&A section of the debate. Has anyone got any questions on driverless …

UNIT 5

🔊 Lesson 5.1 Listening, Exercise A
5.1 P = Presenter   E = Emily   H = Harry

P: We continue this month's focus on going green with a look at eco-friendly homes. Emily Montague reports from a green housing renovation project in Guildford.

E: So, Harry, you've decided to make your home much more eco-friendly. What prompted the change?

H: Well, I used to live in a small flat and I moved into this house a year ago. I was shocked when I got my first energy bill. Three months here cost almost as much as I spent in a whole year in my flat! I realise that it's a much bigger place, but I just couldn't believe how much more the bill was.

E: So how did you get started?

H: Well, I did some of the easy things myself first. I put energy-efficient lightbulbs in every room and put new loft insulation in, but I wanted to make a lot more changes. If you come out into the garden, I'll show you what we're working on now.

E: Ah, I can see you're having solar panels installed.

H: We are. By having these, we can produce about 50% of our own energy every year. In the summer, we'll produce more than we need and then we can sell it back to the energy companies. There's something else that's interesting about this roof though …

E: Oh, really? What's that?

H: The company also transformed the roof into a small garden. They put in wild flowers that attract bees. We've had a bee hive put in at the end of the garden and now we produce our own honey. This will make our roof an energy source and a food source!

E: Amazing! Oh, and what's that over there?

H: That's a water butt, but it's not just one for the garden. We've had our toilet system changed. Our toilet now flushes with rainwater. Any extra water comes down here to this water butt for the garden. We save a lot of water this way. These windows are new as well.

E: Aren't they just double-glazing?

H: They are, but they are much more modern and energy efficient. They have a type of glass fitted that reflects energy back into the house. They also have a different type of gas in between instead of air. This helps to further reduce heat loss.

E: I can hear a lot of work going on as well. What else are you having done?

H: You see this box here? It takes heat from the ground into the house. Come into the living room … We're getting underfloor heating fitted. It reduces our energy bills and it looks a lot better than radiators! And, here's the kitchen.

E: Wow! That is one modern looking fridge!

H: I was fed up with throwing out so much food, so I bought this fridge. We order our food online and the fridge knows what we have in. It then recommends food to cook! It's amazing really and we waste less food.

E: I can hear people working upstairs. What are you having done up there?

H: Come up. We're having a new energy efficient shower installed. It limits how long you can shower for and how much water is used. It obviously saves energy and stops water wastage but it also saves time.

E: How so?

H: It switches off automatically once you've used a certain amount of water. It means some people can't spend all morning in the shower!

E: Not sure I'm too keen on that idea! Any other plans?

H: Yes, we need to get the walls better insulated. I want to use a natural product though, so we're just waiting for it to be delivered. We're also getting a smart meter installed. Hopefully, it'll help us keep an eye on how much – or how little – energy we're using!

E: Thank you, Harry, for showing us around your home. I have to say it looks amazing!

🔊 5.2 Listening, Exercise B
5.7 P = Presenter   A = Agatha   T = Tim   B = Bernie

P: For centuries, man has been obsessed with the idea of going to Mars. Indeed, for a long time, our little red neighbour was the focus of almost all science fiction but now for some it might become a reality. We spoke to three of the Mars One candidates hoping to take part in the first manned mission to Mars. I caught up with one of the candidates, Agatha Nowak, in the library of her university. Agatha, nice to meet you. Why do you want to sign up?

A: Well, partly this will be a break, you know, a break from the usual day-to-day stuff. Like tidying, shopping, studying … Also though, I'm a PhD student and I think it's important to advance science whenever the opportunity presents itself. To me, the Mars One project is exactly this kind of opportunity. The technological advancements made after the moon landings were amazing and I think this project could have the same effect.

P: But this is a one-way ticket. You'll never come back to Earth! Isn't that scary?

A: It is, but I'm also really excited.

P: So, why do you think you would be a good candidate?

A: I'm a really positive person with a lot of energy. I work really well as part of a team and get on with everyone. That's going to be key.

P: Surely, being a scientist is the most important thing you bring to the team?

A: I don't know. Perhaps. Being a scientist isn't enough, you need to be able to live in a small space with other people for a very long time! We can't, you know, just pack up and leave if we're not happy.

P: True! How are you preparing yourself for it?

A: Can you prepare yourself? I don't know. One guy I know is eating just dried and tinned food to get used to the lack of fresh things. I'm not sure that's a great idea. We need as many nutrients as possible before we go!

P: What are you expecting when you first land on Mars?

A: A lot of hard work! We'll have limited food. We'll have to eat dried and rehydrated food at first. Once we establish a community, I think we'll have to attempt to grow our own food, which is going to be challenging. And we also need to build somewhere to live. I've watched people try to build a shelter in the wild on TV and they really struggle. Imagine trying to do it in a spacesuit!

P: What are you going to miss most?

A: I really appreciate drinking a good cup of coffee every morning. Can anyone live without coffee? I read about the coffee machine on the International Space Station, so I'm hoping we get one!

P: Another candidate hoping to join the mission is Tim Davis. Tim loves to challenge himself and is hoping this will prove the ultimate challenge.

I: Shall we take a short break?

T: Sure.

P: How far will you run later?

T: Just a short 30K run. Nothing too hard.

P: That sounds pretty far to me!

T: Not really. I've run lots of marathons and a few ultramarathons. I'll never forget running across the Sahara Desert for seven days. I've always tried to challenge myself physically. I've climbed the tallest mountains in three continents of the world.

P: You like a challenge then?

T: Who doesn't enjoy a challenge? There aren't many left for me on this planet, so why not go to another one?

P: Are you worried or scared at all?

T: Why would I be scared? There's risk in everything we do, and people are just bad at assessing it. Some people worry about flying but you're much more likely to die driving to the airport.

P: True. So, you seem very driven.

T: I am. Everyone wants to leave their mark behind, don't they? Most people choose to have children as their legacy. This will be mine. I'm going to Mars to be a part of history. I'm excited, not scared.

P: What are you going to miss?

T: Well, probably just the simple things in everyday life. I'll miss my friends and family loads. I'll definitely miss fresh food and just being able to pop to the shops to buy something whenever I want.

P: Are you ready?

T: As ready as I'll ever be. I'm not worried about the physical aspect, but emotionally I think it's going to be tough.

P: The last candidate I spoke to is 50-year-old Bernie Johnson. Bernie is an environmentalist from the south of England. When I caught up with him, Bernie was doing a bit of last-minute shopping.

B: … yeah, maybe. Can you pass me a bag?

P: Sure, here you go. So, why do you want to sign up anyway? It's such a long way.

B: It's vital for the future of humans! We have to learn to live independently of planet Earth. The world is not going to end anytime soon, but we have made a real mess of things.

P: Why do you think we've been so terrible?

B: Well, you know, we've made a mess of Earth! We've used loads of natural resources, driven species to extinction and chopped down most of the forests of the world!

P: So, what are you doing to prepare yourself for the mission?

B: I'm trying to live a more isolated life. Some people get really stressed when they forget to take their phone with them. I'm turning off my phone, and permanently disconnecting the internet. For my holiday this year I'm not going away anywhere … I'm staying at home for a month.

P: Is that why you're buying a lot of tinned and dried foods?

B: That's right. I'm going to spend a month not talking to anyone apart from my wife. I'm buying enough food to last for four weeks and we aren't going to leave the living room.

P: Is your wife happy with that?

B: Well, she'd rather be going to Greece or somewhere nice, but, you know, she supports me. It's going to be difficult to live just inside one room, but I think it will be great preparation. I have promised her an amazing holiday next year to make up for it!

I: And how does she feel about you going to Mars?

B: Actually, she seems pretty happy about it …

P: Fair enough. So, if you did get selected, what would you miss about Earth?

B: Well, my wife, obviously. But in general, I think I'll miss being connected to other people. Our world is so small now, really. When you feel lonely you can pick up your phone to connect with loads of people in seconds.

P: True. Anything else? Like food or something else?

B: Um, I don't know. Actually, yes. Strangely, I think I'll miss everyday noises. I'm used to living in a big city and there are so many sights and sounds to keep you stimulated. In space, all you can hear is endless silence. That could be quite disturbing!

Macmillan Education Limited
4 Crinan Street
London N1 9XW

Companies and representatives throughout the world
Language Hub Upper Intermediate Student's Book A
ISBN 978-1-380-04644-4
Language Hub Upper Intermediate Student's Book A with Student's App
ISBN 978-1-380-04638-3

Text, design and illustration © Macmillan Education Limited 2020
Written by Louis Rogers

First published 2020

Designed by emc design ltd
Illustrated by Daniel Limón (Beehive illustration) pp 44, 45, 50, 52, XVI, XVIII, XX, XXII
Cover design by Restless
Cover photograph by plainpicture/Westend61/Uwe Umstätter
Picture research by Emily Taylor

Authentic video footage supplied by BBC Studios Distribution Limited
Café Hub videos produced by Sharp Focus

The authors and publishers would like to thank the following for permission to reproduce their photographs:

Alamy/Art Directors p54(cm), Everett Collection Inc p43, Kertu Saarits pp54–55; **BBC Studios Distribution Limited** p46; **Corbis** p31(knife); **Getty Images** pp15(3), 16(d), AFP p10, Ajr images pXXI(tr), Aluxum p29(6), Cecilie Arcurs pXXI(tl), Atsushi p20(cr), Aurora Open p31(bl), Ezra Bailey p32(b), Thomas Barwick p15(6), Leland Bobbe pXXI(br), Dan Brandenburg p3, Niels Busch pXXIV, Peter Cade p4(tr), Caiaimage pp14, 38(c), Cultura RF pp41, 53, Peter Dazeley pp39, 58–59, Digital Vision p15(2), E+ pp16(a), 32(tr), 38(b), Flashpop p8, Jamie Garbutt pXXI(bl), Geber86 p19(tr), Alexander W Helin p49, Hero Images p37, Hulton Archive Creative p40(tr), iStockphoto pp4(tl), 16(f), 18–19, 20(t), 31(phone, fishing kit), Jupiterimages p33(bm), Ulla Lohmann p25, Jacob Lund Photography pXXIII, Dave Kotinsky p7, John Lamb pp10–11(background), Mikolette p32(tr), Morsa Images pp46–47(background), XXI(cr), Aleksandar Nakic p38(a), National Geographic Creative p28(3), National Geographic Magazines p28(4), National Geographic RF p34, Rick Neves p28(2), Lauri Patterson p16(b), PeopleImages p33(bl), Peter Mason Photography p15(4), Ian Ross Pettigrew p20(cl), Martin Poole p58(tr), Real444 pp6–7(background), RooM RF p13, Asahi Shimbun p27(tr), Marco Siori/EyeEm p31(lighter), SolStock p5(tl,b), Alexander Spatari p22(br), Steve Cole images p17, Michael Stewart p6(tr), Stocktrek Images pp56–57(b), Svariophoto p16(e), Karwai Tang p6(tl), Tetra images pXXVI, Towfiqu Photography p16(c), Urbancow pXXVII, Klaus Vedfelt p1, VisualCommunications p28(1), Dennis Wagner/EyeEm p51, AJ Watt pXXI(cl), Wilpunt p15(5), Dong Wenjie p33(br), Martin Zwick pp34–35(background); **Photodisc** pp22–23, 29(5), 42–43(background), 56(tr); **Reuters Images**/Joe Brock p27(bl); **Rex Features**/Shutterstock/Paul Cooper pXXII; **Shutterstock**/Pressmaster p38(d); **Thinkstock** p31(rope)

Commissioned photographs by Sharp Focus pp11, 23, 35, 47, 59

The author and publishers are grateful for permission to reprint the following copyright material: Extract from 'How Wolves Change Rivers – video' by GrrlScientist. Originally published in The Guardian, 03/04/2014. © 2018 Guardian News and Media Limited or its affiliated companies. All rights reserved. Reprinted with permission of The Guardian, pp50–51.

Printed and bound in Spain

2025 2024 2023 2022 2021
11 10 9 8 7 6 5 4 3